A Wounded ~~Healer~~ Therapist

OrangeBooks Publication

1st Floor, Rajhans Arcade, Mall Road, Kohka, Bhilai, Chhattisgarh 490020

Website: **www.orangebooks.in**

First Edition, 2025

ISBN: 978-93-7426-082-1

Price: Rs. 499.00

Printed in India

A WOUNDED ~~HEALER~~ THERAPIST

WHERE PAIN BECOMES WISDOM, AND STORIES BECOME MIRRORS

ANKUR NAG

Orange Books Publication
www.orangebooks.in

Prelude

This isn't just a book of stories.

It's a mirror, one I am holding out to you, and one I have dared to look into myself.

These pages are not polished masks or carefully rehearsed tales. They are moments when the truth broke through raw, unfiltered, sometimes uncomfortable, always real.

I have learned that healing doesn't come from pretending to be perfect. It comes from daring to be seen exactly as we are flawed, fragile, human.

As you read, you may recognise pieces of your own story.

When that happens, pause. Breathe.

And ask yourself: What mask am I willing to set down?

Let's begin.

Why These Lenses, Why These Stories

I write not just to tell stories, but to see what hides beneath them. Every experience in life, whether joy, shame, anger, or silence, carries layers of meaning. Psychology gives me one lens. Symbolism gives me another. My own lived experience becomes the raw material. Together, these lenses don't explain life fully, but they help me listen to it more deeply.

I use my own life not because it's extraordinary, but because it's ordinary. Each of us walks around carrying wounds, patterns, and questions that shape how we see the world. By sitting with my own moments and examining them honestly, I hope to show that your moments are also worthy of attention. What looks small on the surface, a conversation, a delay, a fight, even a dream, often holds the key to understanding ourselves.

Therefore, vulnerability matters. To analyse your own story requires courage: the courage to admit mistakes, to sit in shame, to say, "Here is my fear, here is my mask, here is my truth." Vulnerability isn't weakness. It's the doorway to connection, because it allows us to drop the performance and meet each other as we really are.

And yet, I hesitate to call myself a "healer." None of us truly heals another. Healing is an inner movement, a shift in consciousness that only the person themselves can allow. At best, I can be a mirror, a witness, a companion who holds space. I can play a part in awakening what is already alive inside the other. But I cannot do their healing, just as no one can do mine.

Perhaps that is the paradox: we are all broken, and it's from within our brokenness that light can pass through. The moment we claim the title of "healer," we risk forgetting that we, too, are still learning, still unravelling, carrying wounds. It isn't our perfection that helps others, but our willingness to remain human with them.

So, if there is one truth I carry through every page, it's this:

We are not *healers*.

We are not *saviours*.

We are fellow *travellers*.

And in the mirror of each other's stories, sometimes quietly, mysteriously, healing happens.

A Note on Sensitive Content

Some stories in this book explore deeply personal, intense, or challenging experiences. They may include thoughts of despair, grief, or even suicidal ideation, as well as unusual spiritual experiences that were real and meaningful to me. They are shared honestly as part of my journey to convey truth, insight, and reflection, not to prescribe any response.

While I believe in the value of facing these truths, I also recognise they may be heavy or unsettling for some readers. Please take care of yourself as you read. If you ever feel overwhelmed, pause. Reach out to a trusted friend, counsellor, therapist, or crisis resource in your area.

This book isn't a substitute for professional care. It doesn't intend to prescribe solutions but to open space for reflection, dialogue, and healing. Take what resonates, set aside what doesn't, and above all, protect your well-being as you move through these pages.

If you find any story triggers distress, discomfort, or difficult emotions, please pause, step back, and care for yourself. Consider reaching out to trusted friends, family, or trained professionals. Here are some general resources:

- Supportive therapy or counselling services if you wish to process complex emotions safely.
- Local mental health services: contact your regional health provider.
- International Suicide & Crisis Hotlines: https://findahelpline.com/

Reading this book is an invitation, not a requirement, to experience or relive any event. Your mental and emotional well-being comes first. You have permission to engage with these stories in a way that feels safe, paced, and supportive.

Acknowledgement

This book wasn't written in isolation.

It was born in the quiet corners of my life, during pauses I didn't choose and silences I had to learn to sit with.

Every story here carries the fingerprints of the people, places, and unseen forces that walked beside me sometimes as *companions*, sometimes as *challenges*, *always as teachers*.

To my parents, sisters, and in-laws—for being both my *roots* and my *mirrors*. You have given me the love that steadies me, and the friction that shapes me. I carry my *courage* from my mother and the *imagination* that fuels this writing from my father.

To my friends—the ones who stayed through the storms and the ones who came only for a season. Each of you, in your own way, has left stories in my heart worth telling.

Special thanks to Rajneesh Kumar, the first reviewer of this book, for his time, insight, and encouragement.

To my teachers, guides, and therapists (my wife), thank you for handing me *the right question at the right time*, for showing me the landscapes within myself I would have never dared to explore alone.

To my clients and students—thank you for showing me my own reflection and polishing me along the way of this healing journey.

To my readers, some of whom I know, most of whom I will never meet—thank you for holding space for these pages. Thank you for leaning in, for *listening without judgment,* and for allowing my words to walk alongside your own unspoken experiences.

To the *strangers* who briefly crossed my path in coffee shops, in airports, on trains, in waiting rooms. You may not remember our conversations, but they became *threads in this tapestry.*

And to the invisible: the whispers, the symbols, the dreams, the angels, and the strange coincidences. You have been my quiet co-authors, reminding me that life is always speaking, even when I cannot yet understand the language.

Finally, to life itself - for the *heartbreaks, the blessings, the pauses, and the thresholds*.

For letting me fail, learn, and begin again.

For making me both the *storyteller and the story.* This book is my offering back to you.

*Special thanks and love to my wife, **Bell Tran (Trần Nguyễn Hoàng Khánh Ngọc)**, for shaping this book with me—for her thoughtful edits, reflections, and even our spirited fights that brought greater clarity and depth. For walking beside me through every step of its creation. In truth, she is the unseen co-author of these pages.*

Authors Note

I didn’t set out to write a book.

I set out to make *sense of my life*.

These stories were never meant to be “chapters.” They began as scattered reflections, moments scribbled on scraps of paper, notes in my phone, voice memos recorded at odd hours. They were simply my way of holding on to something I didn’t want to lose: the feeling, the insight, the truth of a moment before it faded.

Over time, I noticed a pattern. Each story wasn't just about *what happened*, but about *what it revealed*. A fight wasn't just a fight; it was an unspoken fear. A delay wasn't just a delay; it was a hidden need for control. A dream wasn't just a dream; it was a conversation with a part of myself I had long ignored.

I wove in *psychological and / or symbolic interpretations,* not as lectures, but as lenses. The human mind fascinates me, the way our past shapes our present, the way *unconscious patterns repeat,* the way meaning can hide in plain sight. I drew from psychology, spirituality, and lived experience, not to “explain” life, but to deepen the way we listen to it.

This isn't a *self-help manual.*

It's a mirror.

Some reflections will feel familiar. Some may challenge you. Others may simply sit quietly with you until you’re ready to hear them.

If there’s one thing I hope you take away, it's this:

Your *life is already speaking* to you through events, relationships, patterns, and even accidents. The more you pay attention, the more you'll see that nothing is random, and every moment, no matter how ordinary, carries a message.

These are my messages. My echoes. My conversations with life.

I offer them to you, hoping that they may help you recognise your own.

Love,

Ankur

How to Read This Book

Every story you will read here is born out of a lived experience: sometimes an accident of chance, sometimes a struggle between me and my mind, sometimes a gift life handed me, often wrapped in pain so that I could evolve.

I am not a Buddha yet. I am a traveller on the path of the *Bodhisattva*, still learning, still struggling. A disciple once asked a master, "What is the difference between an ordinary man and a Buddha?" The master replied:

A Buddha naturally manifests the perfected virtues and noble characteristics of enlightenment. An ordinary man must make an effort to reflect them. A Bodhisattva, who is still on the journey, remembers again and again to act from compassion, even when anger or fear arises.

If a motorbike swerves recklessly in front of you, you might curse in frustration. A Bodhisattva pauses, breathes, reminds himself: *I am on the path; let me respond differently*. But a Buddha? He doesn't need reminding. Compassion flows from him naturally.

These stories are records of my own reminders, my own struggles with the mind, my own small attempts to be a Bodhisattva. And I know you have your struggles too. You may not voice them, but they live within you, quietly shaping your choices. I hope that when you read these pages, your own *hidden thoughts* will rise to the surface, and you will see them more clearly without *judgment*, without *fear*.

After each story, I invite you to take a **Sacred Pause**. Breathe deeply. Place a hand on your heart, or your belly. Sip some water, some tea, or simply sit by a window and look outside. Ask yourself gently: *When have I felt this? What memory does this awaken in me?* Allow yourself to acknowledge those thoughts, to sit with them, to accept them. That in itself is the first step toward healing.

Each story is followed by:

The Psychological Lens – a way to see the hidden workings of the mind. I use established *psychological concepts,* not to make it academic, but to help you realise you are not alone. These patterns live within many of us.

AND/OR

The Symbolic Lens – a spiritual perspective that reveals what an object, event, or moment might point to. Life often speaks to us through symbols.

But remember, your interpretation is just as valid as mine. If a story stirs something in you, if your own meaning arises, that is your *truth. Trust it.*

Sometimes you may wonder: *But where is the solution? How do I heal this?*

The answer is: sometimes you don't. Sometimes you simply accept. *Acceptance itself is healing.*

Osho once told a story: A man lost a needle in his room. People asked him where he had lost it. "Outside, on the road," he said. So, they all searched outside. But of course, the needle wasn't there. Our thoughts are like these needles lost inside us, while we keep searching outside. Some thoughts are simply meant to come and go. You don't always need to find their meaning. Sometimes just acknowledging them is enough.

For some readers, these pages may be just stories. That is fine. Enjoy them, laugh, cry, feel. But there is only one thing I ask you to avoid: **judgment.** If judgment arises, see it as a signpost. Perhaps healing is being asked for.

Because in the end, this isn't just a book of stories. It's an invitation. An invitation to walk alongside me as a *fellow wounded healer*, to look honestly into your own mirror, and to take one step further on your own *path toward wholeness.*

Contents

Chapter One

The Weight of the Mask

"Every wound wears a mask before it bleeds."

1. The Naked King

There once was a king whose kindness was legendary.

He listened to every grievance, settled every dispute, and ensured his people lived in peace.

The kingdom adored him, but they also wondered:

"How can a man carry so much responsibility and still remain so good?"

Rumours whispered of a secret room that the king visited every night.

One evening, a curious courtier hid inside to discover the truth.

The room was bare except for a single mirror.

When the king entered, he removed his crown, his royal robes, and stood silently before his own reflection.

Then, in a low, trembling voice, he prayed:

"God, this is the real me.

I am not only the kind ruler they see.

I make mistakes.

I wear masks.

I have lied.

I have been deceived by my smile.

But this is my truth, and only You and I know it.

I forgive myself... and I ask for Your forgiveness too."

The king wept. Then he composed himself, put on his robes again, and left.

The courtier came to understand that the king's strength came not from perfection, but from the nightly act of facing his flaws and forgiving them.

I don't want to be the kind of person who hides in an empty room to face myself.

I want to be naked not in body—but in soul.

Naked in such a way that you can see every scar, every wound, every truth I have carried.

I want to stand in the middle of the street, in the market, in the court of life, and let you see me exactly as I am.

No crowns. No masks. No carefully arranged smiles.

Because if we are honest, we are all naked already.

We are just pretending otherwise.

And pretending is exhausting.

Sacred Pause and Reflections

- What *"masks"* do you wear in daily life, at work, at home, with friends?
- When was the last time you *forgave yourself for being imperfect?*
- If you stood in front of your own mirror tonight, what *truth* would you say aloud?

Psychological Lens

Why do we find the king's story so compelling? Because we recognise ourselves in that empty room.

Every human being lives a double life—not in the dramatic, spy-novel sense, but in the quiet, exhausting way we curate ourselves for public consumption. Psychologists call this our "**persona**", the mask we wear so often we sometimes forget our own face beneath it.

The king in our story wasn't weak in needing that room. He was practising something most of us have never learned: **conscious authenticity**.

Research shows that maintaining a false self doesn't just tire us emotionally, it literally drains our cognitive resources. **Dr. Roy Baumeister's** studies on "**ego depletion**" reveal that the mental energy we spend managing impressions is the same energy we need for willpower, creativity, and genuine connection.

Think about it: Have you ever come home from a social event feeling completely drained, even though you "had fun"? That's the cost of the performance.

But here's what made the king extraordinary: his nightly ritual wasn't about self-flagellation. It was about **integration**.

Carl Jung called this "**shadow work**," deliberately engaging with the parts of ourselves we'd rather hide. The king wasn't dwelling in shame; he was practising what psychologist Kristin Neff calls "self-compassion,"—acknowledging his flaws while still treating himself with kindness.

Most of us do the opposite. We either:

- Pretend we're perfect (*exhausting*)
- Beat ourselves up for not being perfect (*destructive*)
- Avoid looking in the mirror altogether (*dangerous*)

The king chose a fourth path: *radical honesty with loving acceptance.*

Here's the twist that makes this psychologically fascinating: the king's public strength actually *came from* his private vulnerability. This isn't just poetic; It's scientifically documented.

How many times have we nodded along with a 'truth' that felt wrong in our gut? These **collective delusions** are the invisible threads that hold our societies together, and they are also the very things that prevent us from seeing ourselves and our world with clarity. It's a silent agreement to live in a shared lie, and the first step to healing is to break that agreement.

Brené Brown's research with thousands of subjects shows that people who practice vulnerability—who can acknowledge their imperfections—are more resilient, more creative, and more capable of genuine leadership than those who maintain perfect facades.

Why? Because when you're not spending all your energy maintaining an image, you can use that energy for real problem-solving, genuine connection, and adaptive growth.

Today, we live in an age of *curated perfection*. Social media has turned everyone into kings and queens with carefully managed public images. But the psychological cost remains the same, perhaps even higher.

The question isn't whether you have flaws, fears, and contradictions. You do. We all do.

The question is, what are you doing with them?

Are you hiding them in an empty room, letting them fester in darkness? Are you exhausting yourself maintaining a performance? Or are you brave enough to do what the king did—to look honestly, forgive compassionately, and integrate consciously?

The king's story is, ultimately, an invitation. Not to overshare or to abandon all boundaries, but to stop pretending first to yourself, then gradually to others, that you're something you're not.

Because here's the final twist: the people who love you want to love the real you—not the performance. And the people who can only love the performance were not loving you anyway.

The mirror is waiting. The question is whether you're ready to step to its edge.

I am taking that first step by sharing my struggle with my own thoughts.

2. The Mask of Spirituality

Spirituality has been my companion for as long as I can remember.

As a child, I was the one people pointed to in family gatherings and temple circles, the "devoted one." Chanting was my rhythm, my breath.

There were days I would lose myself for hours—seven—sometimes eight—wrapped in mantras like a warm shawl. I once recited the *Hanuman Chalisa* twenty-one times a day, every day, for twenty-one days straight.

Sometimes, I would stumbled upon rituals I had never even heard of, yet slip into their flow as if my soul had always known them. The fascination was… intoxicating.

Spirituality wasn't just a practice; it was my lifeline.

When the world felt unstable, it was the anchor that kept me from drifting.

When my heart felt raw, it was the balm that eased the sting.

But then, slowly, quietly, a humbling truth began to whisper to me:

Is spirituality itself a mask?

My spiritual beliefs became a beautiful, elaborate suit of armour, designed to deflect the sharp edges of my own pain.

When something difficult happened, I'd immediately search for a lesson, a higher purpose, a *'divine timing.'* I'd say, "Everything happens for a reason," but the words felt like a bandage over a gaping wound.

I was so busy looking for the light that I refused to sit in the darkness, and in doing so, I bypassed the very healing I was so desperately seeking.

I was wearing a mask—one that could hide wounds.

A defence I had worn so seamlessly, I didn't *even know it was there.*

It didn't make my chanting less sacred.

It didn't make my devotion less real.

But it made me wonder: *what would happen if I met my pain without the mask?*

If I sat with it, bare and unguarded, with no mantra to steady my hands?

And in that wondering, I felt something unfamiliar—not the safety of ritual, but the raw, trembling air of being completely exposed.

Sacred Pause and Reflections

- When life feels painful, what *"masks"* or *defences* do you reach for first?
- What part of you still seeks to be seen as *"spiritual"* rather than simply *human*?

Psychological Lens

On the outside, spirituality can look serene—with malas, rituals, sacred chants, and a calm exterior. But beneath that calm, there can be turbulence. This story reflects what psychologists call **spiritual bypassing (John Welwood)**, the use of spiritual ideas or practices to avoid unresolved emotional wounds or painful truths. Instead of healing, spirituality becomes a shield, a polished surface to hide behind.

Through the lens of psychoanalysis, this shield often takes the form of **reaction formation**, a defence mechanism in which the ego unconsciously expresses the opposite of what it truly feels. For example, someone drowning in anger may double down on presenting themselves as endlessly patient and serene; someone terrified of being ordinary may amplify a persona of being "enlightened." In this way, the ego desperately tries to control their identity, building a mask of spirituality to cover the very human chaos beneath.

Jung would call this mask the **Persona,** a socially admired identity. But when the persona becomes too rigid, it disconnects us from the raw, contradictory self underneath. **Carl Rogers** described this split as **conditions of worth**: the belief that "I am lovable only when I appear wise, calm, or saint-like." Over time, the person begins to fear their own shadow, the anger, fear, jealousy, or longing that contradicts the spiritual image. The more tightly the mask is worn, the lonelier it becomes, because others are not relating to *you*, but to your *performance*.

This creates an inner prison. Admiration from others feels hollow because the part of you that aches to be seen, the wounded, messy, ordinary self, remains hidden. The mask garners respect, but it starves intimacy. The irony is stark: in trying to look "spiritual," the ego suffocates the very essence of spirituality, raw presence, authenticity, and compassion.

Healing begins with honesty. The question isn't, "*Am I spiritual enough?*" but "Am *I using spirituality to connect with my humanity, or to avoid it?*"

When practices are no longer armour but pathways, spirituality ceases to be a mask and becomes a mirror. The ego doesn't need to control identity anymore; instead, identity expands to include both the *calm monk* and the *restless child*, both the prayer and the doubt.

True spirituality doesn't eliminate the shadow—it integrates it.

3. Conversations with My Shadow

It started with one of those quiet declarations we sometimes make to ourselves, almost a whisper:

"I need to work on myself."

So, I began chanting for purification, and as anyone who's walked this path knows, once you start inner work, life gets messy.

Old wounds come up and uncomfortable truths rise to the surface like mud stirred from the bottom of a pond.

I reminded myself to continue, reciting the familiar advice:

If you jump into the mud to clean the mud, you will get muddy. That's natural. Only then can the real cleansing begin.

Then an idea struck me.

The best way to know yourself is to ask the people closest to you.

So, I called my first friend.

"Tell me honestly," I asked, "what kind of person am I?"

My friend paused for a moment. "You sure you want to hear it?"

"Yes," I insisted. "Lay it on me."

"You're… *not reachable.*"

Not reachable? I almost laughed, the shock immediately translating into defensive energy. "What are you talking about? I am always there for people!"

"No," she insisted. "You've built such high walls that no one can actually reach in. People see you as *distant*, even if you think you're available."

That one landed like a stone in my chest. *Distant*? Me? I'd always thought I was the humble, kind one.

Still reeling, I called another friend.

"Be honest," I asked, "how do you see me?"

"Do you really want to know?" he replied. "You might not like it."

"I can take it," I said, thinking, *I've already had my first shock from the previous feedback.*

"You're… *not very grateful.*"

"What? Impossible!"

"I am not saying you aren't grateful inside," he clarified. "I am saying you *don't show it.* People can't feel it from you."

I sat there, stunned.

The image I had of myself, humble, kind, deeply grateful, wasn't the image others held.

This realisation wasn't just hard; it was brutal—a confrontation with who I'd been to others, and what I'd been blind to all along.

The conversation began not with a grand realisation, but with a whisper.

"You're a fake," my shadow hissed at me.

"You pretend to be so kind and patient, but I remember every time you wanted to scream, to lash out, to be selfish."

Instead of recoiling, I listened, the shadow was the voice of my unexpressed anger and my unmet needs.

It was the part of me that felt a tremor of jealousy, the part that wasn't always grateful.

And as I stopped fighting it, I saw that it wasn't trying to harm me; it was holding the pain I had refused to feel.

Our conversations became a quiet agreement: I would stop pretending to be *perfect*, and my shadow would stop having to remind me *I wasn't.*

Sacred Pause and Reflections

- What *qualities* or *feedback* from others do you find *hardest* to *accept* about yourself?
- If your shadow—the *hidden* or *denied* part of you, could speak—what would it say?

Psychological Lens

This story isn't just about an inner dialogue; It's about meeting the parts of ourselves we spend a lifetime trying to deny. **Carl Jung** called this the **Shadow**—the collection of traits, impulses, and emotions we disown because they clash with our self-image.

Anger, envy, selfishness, lust, vulnerability, all the things we believe are "unacceptable" get *pushed into this dark cupboard of the psyche*. But repression doesn't erase them; it only forces them to find indirect ways out, through projection, dreams, slips of the tongue, or sudden surges of emotion.

When I began "talking to my shadow," what surfaced wasn't just darkness; it was truth. As Jung reminds us: *"The shadow is ninety percent pure gold."* That gold is the vitality, creativity, and raw humanity we bury along with the traits we fear.

Modern psychology offers another lens through **Internal Family Systems (IFS)**. What we call "the shadow" can be seen as a collection of *exiled parts*, younger, wounded, or shamed aspects of the self that we pushed away to survive. Around them, the psyche organises *protective parts* that try to keep those exiles hidden: perfectionism, detachment, constant helping, or even spirituality. The "conversation with the shadow" is really a conversation with these *exiled* parts, letting the exiles step out of the basement and be heard with compassion.

At its heart, this story reflects the shift from *self-avoidance* to *self-embrace*. For years, I avoided my shadow because I believed that to look at it was to drown in it.

But paradoxically, what we avoid grows stronger; What we embrace begins to soften. In attachment terms, this is the journey from the *false self* (the mask that gains approval) to the *true self* (the raw, flawed, authentic being beneath).

Symbolically, this story is about *integration versus fragmentation*. To live only in light is to live half a life, brittle, one-dimensional. Integration doesn't mean indulging the shadow's impulses but recognising their existence, owning their energy, and consciously redirecting them. Anger becomes assertiveness, envy becomes inspiration, desire becomes intimacy.

On a spiritual level, the shadow isn't an enemy but a teacher. It strips away illusions, demanding radical honesty. Every time we sit with it, we loosen the ego's grip on perfection and touch a deeper wholeness.

The real healing comes not from silencing the shadow, but from saying: *"I see you. You are part of me. And together, we are human."*

4. Torn Paint

When my wife first mentioned that a couch surfer (*Couchsurfing is a community-based hospitality exchange where travellers can stay for free in the homes of local hosts, or simply meet up with people who share a passion for travel and cultural exchange.*) from Italy might be staying with us, my body tensed.

A stranger. In our small two-bedroom apartment.

Worse, a foreigner I'd never met.

She looked at me expectantly.

I answered with silence—not the kind that invites conversation, the kind that closes a door without slamming it.

Silence is a dangerous communicator.

It lets both people believe what they want.

She assumed I'd acquiesced.

I assumed she'd dropped the idea.

Two days later, my son was "attending" an online health class in his room. I peeked in and saw he was playing games on his phone.

Anger flared and I raised my voice. My wife stepped in, her tone calm, diffusing the heat like she always does.

Half-guilty, half-escaping—my son did something I never expected. He went to meet the *Italian couch surfer*, who by then had found another host in the city.

This was the same boy who avoided strangers like the plague—proof that meeting a stranger was preferable to staying at home and facing an angry dad.

He returned beaming.

"You know what I liked most?" he said. "That *the* Mafia are from Italy!"

It wasn't the cultural insight I had hoped for, but something in him had shifted.

The next day, my wife invited the couch surfer for lunch at her mother's house—more space, more people.

I checked his WhatsApp profile picture: unkempt hair, a ragged shirt, and eyes that carried too many stories.

He looked like someone running from something… or *toward* something.

When we met, my walls cracked.

He was warm, curious, and effortlessly respectful. He greeted every woman with genuine kindness. He tried every dish with delight. There was laughter and ease.

Later, we took him on a short city tour. Because he'd had a bad reaction to street food, I suggested a quiet riverside café.

And that's when I saw it, the big tear in his trousers, right near the back pocket.

A small thing.

But it hit me hard.

Here was a man who had travelled to over 15 countries.

He spoke with grace, carried himself with dignity, and treated strangers like old friends—and yet, his trousers were torn.

Over coffee, I asked what he does for a living.

"I was an Amazon delivery driver in Italy," he said.

I stared.

A delivery driver.

Fifteen countries.

Torn trousers.

And here I was—with a stable job, a roof over my head, comfort, and routine—yet still restless, still complaining, still telling myself the story that I needed *more* before I could *do more.*

That day, *the tear in his trousers revealed the tear in my own perspective.*

Sacred Pause and Reflections

- What is one small *crack* or *tear* in your "paint" that you are *ready* to stop *hiding* and begin to heal?
- If the *"torn paint"* in your life were a *messenger*, what truth might it be trying to reveal?

Psychological Lens

Every time my eyes fell on that torn patch of paint, it wasn't just a wall I was looking at—it was me.

The peeling surface whispered: *"This is who you really are beneath the layers you keep adding."* On the outside, I project order, beauty, and competence. Inside, I fear that if people look too closely, they will see the uneven wall, the flaws, the cracks.

Psychologists call this the **self-discrepancy**, the aching distance between who I want to be (the polished wall) and who I actually feel myself to be (the chipped plaster beneath). Each time I see the paint curling at the edges, it mirrors my own inner split: the man I show, and the man I hide.

Part of me also recognises the **impostor syndrome** hidden here. The fear that one day, someone will scrape off the paint and discover what I've always suspected, that underneath, I am unfinished, unworthy, rough. So, I keep repainting—with achievements, with appearances, with smiles. But no matter how many coats I apply, the cracks eventually resurface.

In truth, the torn paint is also my ego's defence, its attempt to control identity. The paint is my mask, my reaction formation, my performance of being "fine." But the wall keeps teaching me: I don't need more paint. I need to stop fighting the surface. The cracks are not my enemy.

And there's more. From a **Gestalt perspective**, the wall feels like an *unfinished Gestalt,* an unresolved experience calling for completion. My eyes keep returning to it because somewhere deep down, I know I haven't closed the loop with parts of myself I've neglected. The paint won't let me look away until I acknowledge what's raw and unfinished within me.

In **psychoanalytic symbolism**, walls often represent *protection*, boundaries, and the separation between self and world.

Torn paint, especially when left unattended, can signify a gradual breakdown of those protective layers. It awakens an unconscious anxiety: *"If the surface is cracking, what's happening underneath?"*

That's why I sometimes feel restless, even dreadful, when I see it. It's my psyche's reminder that what I guard so tightly may already be softening, already dissolving.

And slowly, I realise, what I thought was an imperfection is actually an invitation. The torn paint is my psyche's way of telling me: *stop covering, start seeing.* In the rawness of that wall, I glimpse the possibility that authenticity begins when I no longer need to look perfect, but can above all enjoy life.

5. The Temple and the Dust

I didn't choose my postgraduate studies out of passion; it was more a mix of pressure and my mother's compassion. My mother, seeing me weighed down by repeated failures in competitive exams in engineering, NDA (National Defence Academy), etc, gently pushed me toward it. I joined the semester late, did well in the exams, but the truth was, I was hollow inside.

Around that time, I felt the strange vacuum left by the absence of someone whose presence I had grown so accustomed to. My days carried the shape of that missing person, like a room echoing with the memory of its furniture, the kind that makes your chest feel like an empty room. I didn't have the word *"depression"* in my vocabulary back then, but that's what it was. I had no tools to cope, except surrender.

One day, I stumbled upon an abandoned Shiva temple near my college. I began visiting every weekend, not to chant or perform rituals, but to talk, cry, and sometimes even argue with Him. I swept the floor, cleaned the idols, and tried to bring some order to the neglected space.

The pigeons didn't make it easy. No matter how many times I cleaned, they covered the floor in feathers and droppings again. Still, I returned. Week after week.

One day, after hours of cleaning, I walked back to my college. My clothes were so dusty that the guard didn't recognise me. He blocked my way until I convinced him it was me. It didn't matter much to me, being drenched in dust. In fact, I preferred it. I didn't want people to recognise me. The dust was a good mechanism. It was my way of becoming invisible, a kind of *shield*. It was a visible sign that I had been elsewhere, doing something no one could see or understand.

I didn't have the words for it back then, but I see it clearly now: The dust wasn't making me dirty. It was *polishing* me.

Sacred Pause and Reflections

- Where is your own *"abandoned temple,"* a place or an activity where you can go to *serve*, *heal*, and *find yourself* in a quiet, unnoticed way?
- When have you felt *invisible* to the outside world? Was that *invisibility* a *burden* or a *gift*?

Psychological Lens

This story reveals a profound paradox: sometimes the world sees us at our "*dustiest*" when, in truth, we are the closest to our authentic selves. In the temple, covered in dust, I wasn't pretending, performing, or competing. I was simply serving, and in that service, I felt a deep sense of alignment: *spiritually, emotionally, and personally.*

Psychologists often talk about authenticity as the alignment between one's inner experience and outer expression (**Rogers, 1961**). At college, I wore the mask of a student pushing through computers and career pressures. But in the temple—dust on my skin, broom in hand, I was simply me. What looked humble, even small, from the outside was actually the most expansive part of me inside.

There was also a tension here: I wanted a spiritual path, but I didn't yet know what that really meant. I couldn't pursue the military, I wasn't deeply inspired by computers, and so I unconsciously gravitated to the temple, the one place where my longing for faith could breathe. The act of sweeping wasn't just cleaning; it was a way of holding onto my soul's orientation.

In **Jungian language**, this was my true self breaking through the **persona,** the social mask of student, son, or achiever. The dust wasn't contamination; it was revelation. The temple showed me that authenticity often doesn't shine. It gathers dust, waits in shadows, and only emerges when we are willing to step out of *performance* and into *presence.*

Symbolic Meaning

The temple symbolises sacred ideals: our internal space of devotion, hope, and higher meaning. **Dust**, in many traditions, carries a double meaning: it's both decay ("from dust you came…") and humility ("ashes to ashes…"), reminding us that even the holiest spaces are still part of the earth.

In this way, the dust isn't just an intruder—it's a truth-teller. It humbles the temple, making it real and alive, rather than frozen in an untouchable ideal. Symbolically, noticing the dust can be a spiritual initiation: the shift from loving perfection to loving what is, even when it's flawed.

Ultimately, the lesson is that devotion matures when it survives the loss of illusion. The true temple isn't the one without dust; it's the one we keep returning to, even after seeing it clearly.

6. The Dishes

I stood at the door, laptop bag slung over one shoulder, lunchbox dangling from the other; my mind was crowded with a thousand thoughts as I stepped inside

As soon as I entered, I walked straight to the kitchen and as always opened the fridge first. After staring inside for a while, I shut it again.

While setting my plate for dinner, my mind kept swaying between countless thoughts. Along with feeding my stomach, I was trying to feed a restless mind.

Soon, I wandered back to the kitchen, and my eyes fell on the sink, overflowing with dirty dishes, but it wasn't the plates that broke me—it was what they carried.

"Now I have to do this too?" I muttered aloud. My face tightened with irritation, and my mind grew even more unsettled.

With a restless gaze, I looked at the sink and suddenly felt my life was exactly like this: full of stacked-up seasons, events, and emotions.

So many that if I started taking them out one by one, perhaps an entire lifetime would pass before I reached the bottom.

Placing my hands on my waist, I took a long breath, then picked up a plate. I thought, *life is like this plate. Served to me exactly as it is.*

It doesn't matter whether I eat it with chopsticks, a spoon, a fork, or my bare hands; I still have to eat. That's the truth.

Slowly, one by one, I began washing each dish with soapy foam. At first, it looked as if the mess was only getting worse. But then, when a few drops of water fell on each plate, they began to shine.

A faint smile crossed my face. What is it that's holding me back? Is my mind... like this *grime*, waiting to be cleaned? Maybe all it needs are a few drops of water. Could *love* be those drops? Or is my ego so big that it stops me from washing myself clean?

I thought, perhaps all it takes is a few drops of love and a gentle lather of soapy foam that holds life's experiences—to *polish the heart.*

Slowly, I moved forward, not just washing the dishes but understanding bigger things about life, and in just a little while, the whole kitchen was gleaming.

I placed my hands on my waist again, took a deep, long breath, and said softly—"So... this is what I need to do, right?"

Sacred Pause and Reflections

- How do you carry *resentment*, do you speak it out, *suppress it,* or let it show in other ways?
- What might it look like to transform a routine task into a *mindful* or even *sacred* act, instead of just a *burden*?

Psychological Lens

On the surface, this story is about household chores, but psychologically, it's about something much deeper: *emotional labour* and *unspoken contracts* we carry in relationships.

Emotional labour (**Hochschild, 1983**) refers not only to the physical work done but the mental tracking, planning, and anticipating of needs.

When I caught myself muttering, *"Now I have to do this too?"*, I recognised what cognitive psychology calls *interpretation bias,* the tendency to interpret one partner's action (or inaction) through the filter of our unmet needs or past experiences. In that moment, the dishes were not neutral objects; they became proof of being overlooked, burdened, and taken for granted. That wasn't about my partner. It was about the lens I was looking through.

I've seen this in couples again and again—the dishes are never just dishes. They become symbols. To one person, a dirty sink may represent feeling unsupported; to the other, it may simply be "I'll get to it later." The gap between those interpretations is where resentment quietly brews. Often, resentment in couples isn't about *what* is being done, but about the perceived imbalance in **mental and emotional load**.

There was also an element of **projection** (**Freud**). I wasn't only irritated at the sink, but I was projecting my own inner clutter onto it. My stacked-up thoughts, emotions, unfinished seasons of life… all of that felt mirrored in the piles of plates. What looked like a household mess was actually an externalised version of my inner state. And beneath it, I noticed a very human theme: the need for **fairness and recognition**, behind which so much of a couple's conflicts hide. It isn't about *who washed how many* *dishes*; it's about: *Do you see what I carry? Do you value it? Do you value me?*

As I stood there scrubbing, I realised something important: the sink wasn't just a *trigger*, it was also an *invitation*. Each plate I washed was a practice in reframing resentment into presence. Each drop of water was a reminder that cleansing doesn't only happen in the kitchen. It happens in the psyche, too.

In other words, the dishes became therapy—for the couple, for the self, and for me.

Symbolic Meaning

On a symbolic level, dishes represent the *ongoing maintenance of life*, the never-ending cycle of use, mess, and restoration. Clean dishes can symbolise order and harmony; dirty dishes, the natural entropy of living. The sink becomes a stage where the dance between self and others plays out: who steps in, who steps back, and who decides when "enough" is enough.

Water used to clean the dishes can be seen as a *symbol of emotional cleansing and renewal.* In some spiritual readings, washing dishes mindfully is a metaphor for washing away the day's emotional residue, *for washing the heart, releasing irritation, clearing old resentments, and returning to clarity.* it's a reset not just for the kitchen but for the inner space.

The deeper lesson is that conflict over "the dishes" is rarely about the dishes themselves—life keeps handing us new dishes. The real question isn't *who will wash them*, but *what we will discover about ourselves while we do?*

They are simply the visible surface of invisible dynamics about fairness, love languages, and the ongoing negotiation of partnership.

But behind every mask, there is a silence; and silence carries its own hidden world.

Chapter Two

The Silence of a Hidden World

"Silence heals—but it can also wound."

7. The Listener's Curse

It felt like my phone was cursed—every call carried someone's *pain*, never their *joy*.

It was just another rainy evening when my phone lit up, showing a familiar name, a familiar rhythm.

A client from years ago—someone who had taken three, maybe four sessions, then vanished without closure, like a guest slipping out in the night.

The message began mid-breath: no hello, no setup.

"We're going through a challenging phase and even had some serious conversations about our future. Therapy has started for both of us, and for now, we're taking a short pause until the weekend to decide how we want to continue"

It wasn't a conversation; it was a drop-off—a raw, pulsing bundle of emotion, handed to me like a ticking package.

I sighed—not out of annoyance, but out of recognition. This is how it always happens.

Old clients. Friends. People who once called me their *"light,"* their *"guide."*

They surface when life is splitting at the seams, when a decision teeters on the edge, when they need the final word or the sacred nudge.

I am not their coach anymore.

I am their secret shrine.

The place they visit is only in an emotional emergency.

And while it's flattering in some small way, it's also—*lonely.*

Because they never book a session.

They want a *heart*, not a calendar; a *listener*, not a ledger.

And the truth is, I made it this way.

I answered midnight messages. I gave my ears without asking for energy in return, and held their breakdowns like a priest cradling confessions, never sending an invoice for the weight.

Somewhere along the way, I trained them to believe I would always be there.

Not as a professional.

But as a friend who asks for nothing.

I became a *human sponge*, and my friendships felt less like connections and more like *emotional transfusions*. They would talk, and I'd leave those conversations with a low ache in my chest and the weary knowledge that I had just given away a piece of my own peace for the sake of theirs.

I began to ask myself:

Have I been offering emotional charity and calling it kindness? Have I told myself that money and healing don't belong in the same room?

Or is there some deeper, older wound in me whispering: *Your worth lies in being available, not in being respected.*

And then the most uncomfortable question of all: *Do I secretly feel validated by being the person everyone runs to in crisis?*

Truth has a way of stinging before it frees you.

That night, the rain outside matched the sound in my head, the questions falling drip by drip.

Sacred Pause and Reflections

- What hidden *belief* fuels your listening: Is it *love*, *obligation*, *fear*, or the *need to feel worthy*?
- When do you listen from your *heart*, and when do you listen from *compulsion*?
- How often do you permit yourself to say, "I hear you, and I also need to *protect my own energy*"?

Psychological Lens

I often notice how easily I slip into the role of **listener** outside of formal sessions—friends, colleagues, even strangers sense it, the readiness in my body, the openness in my eyes, the silence that invites their stories to spill out.

This sounds noble, but there is a shadow side. I have come to recognise in myself traces of **Helper's Syndrome**, the unconscious drive to step into the caretaker role, to absorb another's pain as if it were my own. I listen deeply, I offer support, but rarely do I ask, *"Would you like to book a proper session?"* Part of me fears sounding transactional, another part wants to give freely—and yet another fears rejection.

Underneath lies a hidden belief: *"I am valuable only when I help. My worth is tied to my usefulness."* This is the tender root of **Helper's Syndrome**. While it brings compassion, it can also leave me resentful and depleted.

Closely tied to this is what I call the **Listener's Curse**. People assume I am infinitely available. They confide without boundaries, forgetting that listening isn't neutral; every story leaves an imprint. Without limits, the listener becomes a silent container of unresolved pain, an invisible therapist carrying weight never acknowledged.

The unspoken expectation that I will always absorb others' storms. Over time, without reciprocity, it drains the spirit. Psychologists call this **compassion fatigue**, when giving without replenishment leaves one hollow instead of whole.

Looking deeper, I see this pattern's roots. Attachment **theory** reflects traces of an **anxious-preoccupied attachment**: the belief that I am worthy only when I am needed. **Carl Rogers** would call this a **condition of worth:** *"I matter only when I help."* So, listening became not just kindness, but *survival.*

Through the lens of **transactional analysis**, I notice how I slip into the "*Parent*" role, the caretaker, the rescuer, while others stay in the "*Child*" leaning on me for comfort. The contract is silent but clear: *I listen, you value me.* And when that contract falters, the result is resentment, a quiet ache that whispers: *Who listens to me?*

This creates **cognitive dissonance**. My self-image says, *"I am dependable, kind, strong."* But my inner reality sometimes whispers, *"I am tired, unseen, alone."* The very identity that gave me pride becomes a mask, hiding my own longing to be cared for.

The curse *isn't* listening itself. It's forgetting that listening without boundaries isn't love, it's *self-disappearance.*

Healing begins not with silence, but with boundaries, what **Cloud & Townsend** call the sacred art of saying *"no."* And it deepens with *self-validation*: the radical act of remembering my worth doesn't come from the weight I carry for others.

Symbolic Meaning

The "Listener" in this story symbolises *the well*, a deep source of water that others draw from. At first, the water is abundant and life-giving, but without replenishment, the well runs dry.

This represents how people who are naturally empathetic or insightful often become *containers for other people's stories*. The "*curse*" lies not in listening itself, but in forgetting to refill the well, symbolising **self-renewal**.

The absence of reciprocity mirrors *unbalanced scales,* a universal archetype of *injustice* and *imbalance.* The listener's silence becomes both a gift and a burden, just like a sacred vessel that is never allowed to be emptied or cleaned.

8. The Itch of Unfinished Stories

Halfway through the podcast, my chest tightened—not from pain, but from an *itch of unfinished stories.*

I sat down to listen to a podcast on couple relationships, something I truly want to understand more deeply, and it was nearly two hours of wisdom, rich with insights.

But within minutes, I noticed it: the itch.

A restless scan in my mind, looking for somewhere else to be.

Maybe I should tidy the living room.

Or sketch out that new project idea.

Or at least check my emails while the podcast plays quietly in the background. It isn't like I am drowning in tasks.

I've spent hours this week scrolling my phone or staring blankly out the window.

Yet now, in the middle of something that matters, I want to do more.

So, I asked myself:

Why?

Why the constant urge to split my attention?

What am I really chasing?

Because deep down, I know this isn't about "using my time well," or being more productive.

It's something else.

It feels like a subtle discomfort with being *still.*

Like the quiet is too loud.

Like being fully present with one thing might crack open emotions I'd rather leave untouched.

The whispers come:

"Don't waste time."

"Do more."

"Be efficient."

But beneath those voices is another one, softer, almost shy:

What if you just let this be enough?

Maybe this isn't a *time management* problem at all.

Maybe it's a *self-connection* problem.

I am not short on productivity; I am short on *permission*—permission to simply be.

To listen without rushing to the next thing.

To let one experience be *complete* in itself.

So maybe the real practice today is this:

Not *multitasking*. Not *fixing*.

Just sitting fully with one meaningful thing, and letting it change me.

Sacred Pause and Reflections

- What is the *"itch"* you feel when you are trying to be *fully* present with something meaningful? What kind of *distraction* does your mind create to *avoid stillness?*
- If you gave yourself permission to just *be* with one thing today, what would you choose?

Psychological Lens

The restless urge to do something else, even while engaged in an important task, isn't simply about distraction; it's about a deeper conflict of motives. Psychologists call this a form of *dual-attention pull*: one part of the mind wants to be present, the other part keeps whispering, *"You should be doing more."*

A friend once told me how he registered for an online course and let the videos run in the background while answering emails or scrolling on his phone. When I asked why, he said, "I just need the certificate. People will know I've done it." This is a perfect example of what psychologists call **extrinsic motivation (Deci & Ryan, 1985)**, doing something for recognition, reward, or approval. In such cases, attention naturally scatters, because the inner self knows: *"This isn't really for me."*

In contrast, when an activity is fuelled by ***intrinsic motivation***, genuine curiosity, passion, or the desire to grow, the itch quiets down. We listen more fully, engage more deeply, because the task nourishes us.

But the itch also hides something else: a *fear of incompleteness.* Part of me whispers, *"If I only do this, what about all the other things left undone?"* This is why the itch often shows up in listening: even as I hold space for someone, another voice nags, *"Shouldn't you be finishing that other task?"* It's not about priority alone; it's about the fear that stillness or singular focus means loss.

This pattern reflects what researchers sometimes call *performance anxiety* or a *scarcity mindset.* Time and recognition feel scarce, so I try to hold too many threads at once. But ironically, that restlessness prevents true completion.

In that sense, the *itch* isn't a flaw but a clue. It asks me to pause and ask: "*Am I doing this for myself, or just to prove something to others? Am I present because I value this, or restless because I feel trapped in proving my worth?*"

When I answer honestly, the itch itself becomes a mirror, showing me not just *what* I do, but *why* I do it.

The restlessness also reflects the **Zeigarnik Effect**, the psychological tendency for unfinished tasks and unresolved thoughts to intrude upon the present. Each dangling thread in the listener's mind pulls attention away from the conversation, creating an almost gravitational pull toward incompleteness. The more the other speaks, the more the listener's unfinished inner monologue grows louder, tugging them out of the moment.

Edward Hallowell coined the term **Attention-Deficit Trait (ADT)** to describe a modern state of constant partial attention, not a disorder, but a stress-induced condition where the brain mimics ADHD because of overload. In this restless listening, ADT shows itself: the difficulty of sustaining deep attention when the nervous system has been rewired for rapid scanning, interruption, and anticipation.

Our attention doesn't itch because it's weak, but because it craves *completion*.

9. The Corridor and the Clock

Evenings in my village were pure freedom.

The playground was my kingdom, dusted with red earth, ringing with laughter, echoing with the crack of cricket balls. Under the orange sky, time dissolved.

But joy had a deadline: I knew what waited at home.

Our house had a long, narrow corridor—and at the far end, always, always, stood my mother.

With a stick.

Her figure backlit by the warm glow of the house; me at the entrance—dusty, tired, a little guilty—staring back with puppy eyes.

I knew I was late; I knew what came next.

Years later, in the corporate world, I became obsessed with being on time.

Not out of politeness, nor out of professionalism.

But because, deep down, I am still that little boy in the alley… afraid of being punished for being too *alive*, too *playful*, too *free*.

Even now, I reach airports absurdly early.

I am the first to arrive for meetings.

When someone says, "It's fine to be late," I feel heat rise in my chest. It isn't about the clock. It's about safety. It's about fear. It's about that corridor... and that stick.

I am learning now that safety doesn't have to be earned by punctuality.

That joy doesn't have to be punished.

And maybe, just maybe, it's time to walk that corridor again, not toward *fear*, but toward *myself.*

Sacred Pause and Reflections

- Can you recall a moment when the *pressure of time* stole your *presence* from what *truly mattered?*
- How has your *relationship* with your *mother* shaped the way you wait—for *love*, for *answers*, for *healing*?

Psychological Lens

What we feel in adulthood isn't always born in the present moment. Often, it's the echo of something older, a childhood conditioning, or even a thread woven through generations. **Mark Wolynn** calls this **inherited family trauma**, the idea that the fears and patterns we carry don't always begin with us, but may be passed down, encoded in both memory and body.

Sitting in that hospital corridor, the ticking clock may have felt like it belonged to that moment, but perhaps it was also amplifying earlier echoes. Maybe the helplessness wasn't only about the present test results. Maybe it carried the familiar weight of being a child waiting for an adult's verdict, or even the silent anxieties passed down from parents and ancestors who lived through uncertainty, scarcity, or sudden loss. In trauma psychology, this is called **implicit conditioning**, a way the body remembers and reacts, even when the mind doesn't fully know why.

It also ties into environmental cues and emotional conditioning. According to **classical conditioning (Pavlov, 1927)**, repeated exposure to a certain space during emotionally charged moments can cause the space itself to become a trigger. Over time, even neutral stimuli (like a clock ticking) can evoke feelings of tension, urgency, or fear. Psychologists call this **stimulus generalisation**, when the nervous system can no longer separate the old emotional wound from the present environment.

This is why the corridor was so unbearable: it **wasn't** just about waiting; it was about being powerless, about having no control—a feeling my nervous system already knew too well. The corridor was both *real* and *symbolic*. Real in its walls, its clock, its sterile air: Symbolic in how it brought me face-to-face with old imprints of helplessness and the very human struggle with time.

What psychologists call *time anxiety*, that restless awareness of passing minutes, the dread of waiting, is often a mask for something deeper. In my case, the corridor pulled me into the collision between my *adult self*, who wanted to manage and fix, and my *inner child*, who once had no power to change what was coming.

When I look back now, I see the corridor not just as a hallway of dread, but as a **mirror of unfinished stories**. It reminds me that what we feel today might not always start today, and healing sometimes means gently tracing the thread back, until we learn to hold not only our own fear, but the echoes that came before us.

Symbolic Meaning

Symbolically, the corridor represents **life's in-between spaces—** the transitional periods when we are moving from one chapter to another but have not yet arrived. The clock embodies the **relentless measurement of existence**, a reminder that all waiting has an endpoint, whether we acknowledge it or not.

The act of walking through the corridor while the clock ticks becomes a metaphor for **liminality**, a state anthropologist Victor Turner described as being *"betwixt and between"* old and new identities. The discomfort isn't just about the destination; it's about being suspended in a space where control is minimal and awareness is heightened.

The deeper takeaway: when we stop resisting the corridor, when we walk mindfully through it, the clock doesn't become less loud, but its ticking turns from a threat into a rhythm.

10. The Sound of Waiting

My wife sings. She always has—sometimes softly, sometimes with complete freedom and emotion, but always from a place deep within. For her, music isn't a hobby; it's breath.

Lately, she's been swept up in something she's longed for: musical theatre and improv. Rehearsals have been pouring into her days like monsoon rains after a long drought, and I've been watching her bloom.

Tonight, two people from her group came over to rehearse. I could hear the laughter, the shuffling of papers… and then, unexpectedly, the deep, resonant chime of a singing bowl, the same kind we use in healing work.

Ah, I thought. She's moved from rehearsal into offering them *healing*. Of course.

That's when the voices began:

She just wants to feel important.

She's showing off.

She doesn't care that we have not eaten.

She's forgotten her sister's invitation.

They came like knocks on a door I didn't want to answer.

And then, a memory.

Years ago, I was married to someone else. Back then, I used to attend Buddhist group meetings. My own sacred time. I wasn't seeking escape, just a little stillness in a noisy world. But every time I went, I felt a rope around my ankle, pulling me back.

Not my fear, *hers*.

And it came wrapped in accusations: *You're avoiding home. You care more about them than us.*

I began leaving meetings early. Sometimes I wouldn't go at all. And when I did, I'd come home to air so thick with tension, it smothered any peace the chants had given me.

That marriage ended, but apparently, not everything in me did.

Because tonight, standing in my living room, restless and irritable, I realised:

I wasn't just reacting to my wife's extended rehearsal.

I was reacting to the ghost of once being blamed for seeking my own sacred time.

Once, I was the one misunderstood.

Now, I was the one who misunderstanding.

I want to be the supportive partner who celebrates her joy.

But another part of me whispers, *why does she get to be free, when I* wasn't*?*

That whisper isn't cruel. It's ancient. It's the cry of the man who once waited, unseen.

I imagined she wanted to be "important," not because she actually did, but because I once felt unimportant. I imagined she was forgetting me, because I still remember forgetting myself just to keep the peace.

Her joy made my shadow feel exiled. That isn't her fault. That's my work.

If you asked for the short version of tonight's story, I'd say this:

A woman followed her music.

A man heard a singing bowl… and also heard his past.

And in that vibration, healing began, not for those in the room, but for the one standing outside it.

Because sometimes, the person who waits isn't waiting for someone to return from rehearsal.

He's waiting for the part of himself that never got to finish his own *song*.

And tonight, maybe he finally heard it.

Sacred Pause and Reflections

- What *emotions* rise in you during *waiting*, *impatience*, *fear*, *hope*, or *surrender*?
- Do you tend to *fill silence with activity*, or *can you sit with the quiet uncertainty?*
- What might *waiting be teaching you* right now about *trust, patience, or timing?*

Psychological Lens

This is a great example of *projection* and emotional *transference*. My annoyance with my wife's rehearsal **wasn't** just about her current behaviour; it was coloured by a past marriage where my own sacred activities were met with fear, accusation and withdrawal.

In psychodynamic terms, this is *transference*, the unconscious process of re-living emotions from a past relationship and unconsciously transferring them onto a current one. I could feel my mind "*tagging*" her rehearsal with the emotional imprint of old wounds, blurring the line between *then* and *now*.

The tension I felt also reflects **moral dissonance**, the internal friction of holding two truths simultaneously:

"I want to be the supportive partner who celebrates her joy."

"A part of me resents her freedom because I was once denied mine."

This dissonance is intense because it pits the *aspirational self* (the partner I want to be) against the *wounded past self* (the one who felt unseen). In **Internal Family Systems (IFS)** terms, the *"supportive partner"* and the *"neglected past self"* are different inner parts of the psyche, each with its own needs, both valid, both demanding recognition, fighting for space and attention.

There's also a **need for visibility** at play, a deep human need to feel seen and heard, especially when our partner is fully absorbed elsewhere. When that need isn't met, the mind can drift towards **interpretations coloured by old pain**, like *she's showing off* or *she's forgotten me,* even if they're not objectively true.

Finally, this is *shadow integration* in action. My old unseen self, the man who once waited for permission to honour his own sacred time, was finally seen in the present moment.

By observing these inner dynamics rather than acting on them unconsciously, I could turn **irritation into insight**, **projection into awareness**, and **moral dissonance into growth**.

Symbolic Meaning

The *singing bowl* becomes a key symbol here. In spiritual traditions, its vibration represents presence, healing, and clearing of energy. But in this moment, the bowl's chime doesn't soothe; it *awakens* the echo of an old wound.

Symbolically, my wife was following the *"Call to Joy"*; her rehearsal and healing work are rivers flowing outward. I was standing on the *"Shore of Waiting"*, holding a vessel of my own unexpressed needs. The *"sound of waiting"* is both literal (the singing bowl's resonance) and metaphorical: the hum of an old story still vibrating inside.

This moment could also be framed as the **role reversal archetype**, once the seeker yearning for understanding, I now unknowingly stepped into the role of the one withholding it. In mythic terms, it's the *mirror stage of relationships*, where a partner's freedom reflects your own *unfinished liberation*.

11. When the Silence gets too Loud

Today, my mind feels like a *marketplace at rush hour*—noisy, chaotic, full of voices that demand, accuse, distract, and dissolve.

It has been four months without work in Vietnam.

Four months of waking up to unfinished thoughts, and brushing hope off my shoulders like dust that never leaves.

This morning, I cooked—maybe to feel useful, just to hold onto a thread of routine.

Then I let a movie play in the background while I dozed in and out.

I told myself I was resting, but really, I was hiding from myself, from the voice that keeps saying: *"You should have figured it out by now."*

All day, a conversation has been building in my chest:

I want to go to India: to help my father finish the leftover construction work, to change the air, and to change the energy.

But the words are stuck; I couldn't say it to my wife.

When should I say it?

How should I say it?

Will she think I am escaping again?

My wife has been quiet today. Not cold, just quiet in that way she gets when she's giving me space.

I know it's kindness.

And yet, some part of me twists it into something else—like she's gotten used to this quieter version of me, the one who doesn't bring home good news anymore.

Then a darker thought strikes:

"Am I angry because she's not worried about finances?

Is going to India really about opportunity, or do I just want to provoke her?

Do I want her to miss me, to fear for me, just so I know I still matter?"

The thought lands heavily.

Is this *narcissism?*

Does it start here, not with vanity, but with a *hunger for reaction?*

Am I fading from my own reflection, and reaching for someone else's eyes to prove I still exist?

It's a cry for *significance* in the middle of a long emotional drought. It's the body's protest when it feels unseen for too long. It's *attention-seeking*, not as manipulation, but as *survival.*

We are wired to want resonance.

When a man loses his work, he often loses the script he was taught to live by: *provide, perform, protect*.

When that script disappears, what's left is the quiet terror:

Will anyone still see me if I am no longer delivering value?

I don't know yet if going to India is an escape or healing.

I don't know yet if my silence is grace or fear.

But I do know this:

My anger isn't the enemy. My thoughts are not betrayals. They are messengers.

They're saying:

You want to feel needed again.

You want someone to reach in and say: You matter. Not because you earn. Just because you exist.

And perhaps… that someone, first, has to be me.

Sacred Pause and Reflections

- Have you ever experienced a *silence* that *felt heavy, uncomfortable*, or *even unbearable?* What was *beneath it?*
- What *unspoken emotions* or *memories* come to the surface for you when things get *too quiet?*
- How can you begin to practice being in a space of *"silence,"* even when it feels *uncomfortable*? What kind of *inner wisdom* might be waiting for you there?

Psychological Lens

Silence can be soothing, even sacred; but silence can also be suffocating. In my story, silence **wasn't** peace; it was *pressure.* What made it unbearable **wasn't** the absence of sound, but the *presence of everything unspoken.*

This story is really about what **Eric Berne** (Transactional Analysis) called *significance hunger*, the deep human need to feel *visible, valued, and acknowledged* through "strokes" of recognition. When silence replaces acknowledgement, the mind doesn't sit still; it begins searching for proof of mattering. Sometimes that means provoking conflict, sometimes withdrawing as in my case, asking internally: *"Do I want her to miss me? Or even to fear for me? Just so I know I matter?"*

From an **attachment perspective**, this is the anxious-preoccupied pattern surfacing. When emotional security feels threatened, especially in moments of vulnerability, like my unemployment, the need for reassurance grows louder. What looks like irritation at silence is, at its core, a craving for emotional proof of worth.

At one point, I even wondered: *"Is this narcissism?"* But what was present wasn't narcissism in the clinical sense. It was a bid for connection at a time when my professional identity, and with it, my usual anchors of self-esteem, had collapsed. When our external roles (provider, achiever, doer) are stripped away, the sense of self can shrink until it relies almost entirely on others' validation. Psychologists call this **external validation dependency**, but experientially, it feels like leaning on silence, desperate for it to speak back.

There's also **Viktor Frankl's** idea of the **existential vacuum** at play. The loss of work didn't just create financial worry; it created a void of meaning. In that void, every silence from my partner became amplified, echoing the deeper question: *"Who am I, if I am not functioning, producing, or providing?"*

And when silence happens inside a partnership, it carries another meaning: if one partner cannot express what they feel, the relationship itself starts carrying the weight of that unspoken absence. Silence is rarely neutral in intimacy; it's interpreted. It can be heard as distance, rejection, or lack of care, even if it comes simply from the partner's own overwhelm or inability to articulate. In healthy partnerships, silence can be grounding and safe. But when it's tied to unmet needs and unspoken fears, it becomes a *wedge*: one person feels invisible, the other feels pressured, and the bond quietly strains under the weight of words unsaid.

In this way, the silence wasn't just quiet; it was a *mirror*. A mirror that reflected my unmet hunger for significance, my anxious need for strokes, and my struggle to find meaning when the old definitions of identity had fallen away.

Symbolic Meaning

The *"silence"* in the story is more than the wife's quiet; it symbolises the **mirror gone blank**. I used to see my reflection (worth) in others' responses. Without that mirror, there is an existential echo chamber where doubts grow louder.

The idea of *"going to India"* functions symbolically as a **flight impulse**, not necessarily an escape from marriage, but from the current self-image of stagnation. India here can be read as an archetypal **return to the father** (literally helping his father with construction work), a move toward grounding and rebuilding identity from a place of origin.

The "cry for significance" is the central motif. In symbolic psychology, it aligns with the **Wounded King** archetype, a leader without a kingdom, searching for confirmation that he still matters even without the crown (job, income, status).

The resolution hinted in the final lines, *"That someone has to be me"*, is a movement toward **self-sourced validation**. In Jungian terms, it's the beginning of integrating the **Self** as the inner authority, instead of depending on relational mirrors for worth.

12. The Visit and the Silence

Tonight, an old friend came over for dinner—once, he was the one who called me almost daily, hungry for clarity, eager for guidance, leaning on me like a compass he trusted.

But tonight, he arrived with a different energy.

He spoke in long, sweeping declarations about how his thinking had evolved, how he could now predict events before they happened, and how his *kundalini* energy had reached its peak and given him complete control over his life.

I listened.

Not because I agreed.

If I am honest, I was stunned.

Really? I thought. *The energy meant to still you, to align you, is making you restless and loud?*

But I didn't say that.

I said nothing.

And that nothing followed me long after he left.

Why was I silent?

Was it because I am standing in one of the lowest valleys of my life and feel I've lost the right to speak? Was it because I've grown calmer and no longer feel the need to correct others?

Or… was it because I feared my words wouldn't land, wouldn't carry weight, without the visible armour of "success—*money, position, power?*

Do people only listen when wisdom is draped in status?

Or am I the one diminishing my own voice because I am vulnerable right now?

I don't know the full answer.

But I do know this, tonight, my silence spoke more to me than his words ever could.

It told me where my doubts are still hiding.

It told me that the voice I am afraid is gone—is only waiting for me to claim it again.

Sacred Pause and Reflections

- Do you sometimes use *silence* as a *shield*, to protect yourself from *conflict* or *vulnerability*?
- Have you ever felt *humiliated* or *left behind* because others found *success* and *moved ahead*, while you were still struggling to find your place? What did that moment reveal about how you measure *your own worth?*

Psychological Lens

For me, this story isn't really about my friend's proclamations; it's about my silence, and what that *silence* revealed. Psychologically, I can see how **social comparison theory** (**Festinger, 1954**) was at work. I wasn't doubting my wisdom; I was doubting whether my wisdom "counted" without the external badges of credibility, money, power, and visible success.

This dynamic is closely linked to the **impostor phenomenon**: the tendency to discount one's competence when the external picture of success doesn't match the internal reality. My friend's loud proclamations about spiritual mastery became a mirror, pulling me into an unconscious comparison that made me question my own authority to advise.

What's important here is my **self-silencing** pattern. Psychologist **Dana Jack** describes self-silencing as a defence mechanism often rooted in fear of conflict, loss of connection, or rejection. My silence wasn't pure acceptance; it was partly avoidance, a way of protecting myself from potential invalidation. In this sense, silence became less about wisdom and more about protection.

From a communication perspective, there is also **status bias** at play: the human tendency to assign authority not by substance but by appearance, confidence, success, and charisma. In doubting my own voice, I was internalising this bias, as though my words needed external proof before they could carry weight.

Underneath all of this lies a tension between my **Persona** (the social mask of being accomplished, confident, spiritually "together") and my deeper **Self** (the authentic source of insight that exists regardless of circumstance). That night, my silence showed me how much I was still equating wisdom with status, and how much of my voice was waiting to be reclaimed, even in the absence of worldly armour.

Symbolic Meaning

Symbolically, this evening unfolded like an encounter between archetypes. My friend embodied **The Magician in Shadow**, power proclaimed, mastery declared, but ungrounded in humility. I, in contrast, embodied **The Hermit**, lantern in hand, wisdom intact, but retreating rather than stepping forward.

The silence itself functioned as a **mirror**, reflecting both my restraint and my doubt. In some spiritual traditions, silence is the highest form of listening, a vessel for deeper truth. Yet it can also become a form of **invisibility** when it's rooted in self-diminishment. The test that evening wasn't about whether I could prove my friend wrong; it was about whether I could stand in my own authority without the trappings of success.

The "visit" itself became symbolic of a test: *Will someone like me stand in their own authority even without the trappings of success? Or will they wait for external validation before reclaiming their voice?*

The deeper lesson is this: wisdom doesn't vanish when circumstances crumble. It isn't diminished by valleys, nor amplified by peaks. It simply waits, steady, to be spoken again.

Yet silence doesn't only comfort or wound,
it also gives birth to something deeper,
darker: shame.

Chapter Three

Shame

"Shame is the silent thief of worth; it hides in the shadows until named."

13. The Fear of Empty Plates

I think I finally know what my biggest fear is.

It isn't a failure.

It isn't rejection.

It's this:

That I will lose every rupee I have… and one day, sit in front of *an empty plate with nothing to eat.*

There. I said it.

On paper, it looks dramatic. In my body, it feels like *the truth.*

Like a quiet storm that hums under my skin, patient, invisible, always ready to break.

Today, my sugar level spiked to 340—that's how much this fear is eating me alive.

No income.

No stability.

Just the low hum of panic running under every thought, every plan, every dream.

I am not sure I've ever felt this low. So, I asked myself the question I didn't want to face:

"What am I going to do about it?"

And for a moment, there was no answer.

That was the scariest part.

Then a wild thought burst in:

"What if I just spend it all?"

"What if I buy gifts for everyone I've ignored, travel to the places I've always wanted, burn the script completely... and see what happens? let me be head on with this fear"

It wasn't joy speaking.

It was *defiance*, a desire to stare the fear in the face by doing the exact thing it warned me not to do.

For a brief second, it felt thrilling.

But then another voice whispered:

"Is this courage, or is panic merely acting under the guise of bravery?"

That question stopped me cold.

What I want is freedom from the grip of fear.

I want to wake up without rehearsing disaster in my head.

I want my self-worth to stop being measured in digits.

So, I slowed down.

I breathed.

I sat in the kind of silence that doesn't give answers, but clears the fog.

And in that space, something simple came through:

I don't have to destroy everything to feel free.

I just need to stop letting fear run the show.

Maybe I can:

Give one person something meaningful, not to escape fear, but to practice *love.*

Visiting somewhere close brings me joy, not as an escape, but as an act of *aliveness*.

Create a small "Fear Fund", a sum set aside to remind my nervous system: *You are safe.*

I don't have all the answers.

I am still afraid.

But I am learning this,

Peace doesn't come from emptying the bank account.

It comes from emptying the fear.

Sacred Pause and Reflections

- What is your deepest fear about "*not having enough*"?
- What are you most *afraid will happen if the money runs out?*

Psychological Lens

At first glance, this story looks like it's about food, but it isn't about hunger at all. It's about survival, scarcity, and the deep psychological imprints that form when life teaches you that *emptiness is dangerous*. In psychology, this often connects to what we call a **scarcity mindset**, the constant fear that there will not be enough, that resources will vanish, that security is fragile. It lingers long after the actual danger is gone.

This fear of empty plates is rarely about the plate in front of you; it's about the plate in your memory. Perhaps, in childhood, there were moments when food, love, or safety felt uncertain. The mind, brilliant at protecting us, holds onto those imprints. Even years later, with abundance around, the body reacts as if famine is always near. This is how **trauma memory** works: the nervous system keeps responding to the past as though it were still present.

It also ties into **object relations theory**. The plate itself becomes symbolic of care, nurturing, and availability. An empty plate doesn't just mean no food; it unconsciously signals, "*You may not be cared for.*" This is why the reaction is so strong. It isn't logic, but *attachment fear*. Psychologists studying **attachment anxiety** describe this exact phenomenon: the panic that what sustains us (whether food, love, or attention) might disappear at any moment.

Inside me, the conflict feels like **cognitive dissonance**. On one hand, I know intellectually that the fridge is full, the cupboards are stocked. But emotionally, the sight of emptiness makes my chest tighten, as if I am about to be left alone without support. The child in me and the adult in me are living in two separate realities.

The scarcity is that it doesn't end when the plate is filled. Because what it really fears isn't hunger, it fears abandonment. And no amount of rice, bread, or curries can fill that space. Healing begins when I stop trying to silence that fear with food or control, and instead meet it with compassion. As psychologists working with **inner child healing** suggest, I must turn toward that frightened child within me and say: *You are safe. You are seen. You will not be left empty again.*

Scarcity doesn't begin in the wallet; it begins in the nervous system.

14. The Bread of Shame

I've always considered myself *blessed*, so blessed that much of my life has been shaped by gifts.

Clothes.

Books.

Watches.

Once, even the underwear I wore had been a gift from someone.

I remember one moment from college with startling clarity.

We had been told that students facing financial hardship could apply for a fee concession. My family wasn't well-off, so I applied.

I sat in front of the interviewer, telling him the truth, that we were struggling.

He listened, then let his gaze drift down to my clothes.

"How much are your pants? Your shirt? That watch? Those shoes?"

I told him they were all gifts from relatives, given during a family ritual called *janayu* (Upnayan thread ceremony) when I turned sixteen.

He didn't believe me.

The application was rejected.

For years, I lived in the warmth of other people's generosity. I became so accustomed to receiving that I forgot the art of *giving*.

I didn't know how to buy a gift for someone else, not because I didn't want to, but because it had never been my role.

Then life shifted. Money took a sabbatical from me.

The gifts still came. But now, they felt different.

The same packages that once made me feel loved began to carry a quiet weight.

*I felt it in the food my in-laws sent home.

*In every neatly wrapped parcel from a friend.

*An invitation to a birthday party felt heavy on me.

*In every well-meaning gesture that now tasted faintly of *pity*.

Sacred Pause and Reflections

- When have you felt *uncomfortable receiving* something, whether *love*, *help*, or *gifts*?
- Do you sometimes equate "receiving without giving" with weakness or unworthiness?
- How does shame still show up in your life, and what is one small act of *vulnerability* you can take to begin to *heal it?*

Psychological Lens

In **Kabbalistic** teaching, the "bread of shame" (*nahama de kisufa*) is described as the unease of receiving blessings without labour. From a psychological perspective, this unease reflects a tension between **deservingness** and **self-worth**. **Carl Rogers** would say it's the conflict between our *real self* (worthy, whole, loved as is) and our *ideal self* (only acceptable if we earn, achieve, perform). When life offers grace without transaction, the ego panics, because its control mechanism: *earn to be loved*, no longer applies.

On the surface, shame looks like a private emotion, a blush, a downward gaze, the tightening of the body when we feel exposed. But "the bread of shame" points to something deeper: the discomfort of receiving without earning, of taking in love, gifts, or abundance when the inner self whispers, *"I don't deserve this."*

Psychologists often link this to **imposter syndrome**, the inner conviction that success or affection is unearned, a fraud waiting to be revealed. Yet it also connects with **learned helplessness** and **internalised shame**, where early conditioning creates the belief that worth must always be proven through struggle. When something comes freely, it feels unsafe, even contaminating. Instead of savouring bread, the mind insists it's bitter.

Helen Block Lewis (1971) described shame as a **self-conscious emotion**, one that arises not from external punishment, but from how we evaluate ourselves in the eyes of others. Unlike basic emotions (anger, fear, joy), self-conscious emotions require self-awareness. They are about *who we think we are*, not just what happened. This makes shame uniquely destabilising: it doesn't say *"I did something wrong"* but *"I am wrong."*

And yet, there is another side. Scholars of emotion remind us that shame also has an **adaptive function**. At its healthiest, shame is the inner compass that pulls us back into relationships, reminding us that we are connected to others. It's meant to protect bonds, not destroy them. The tragedy comes when shame becomes chronic and toxic, when it no longer nudges us toward connection but convinces us that we are unworthy of it.

At its core, this dynamic is tied to **conditional love**. If, as children, affection was linked to achievement, obedience, or sacrifice, we learn the silent equation: *"I am valued only when I give, perform, or endure."* As adults, receiving freely feels like a violation of that equation. Gratitude gets tangled with guilt. Pleasure becomes contaminated by a fear of unworthiness. The inner critic whispers: *"You didn't work hard enough. You don't deserve this gift, this love, this ease."*

The irony is that shame starves us of the very nourishment we long for. The bread is always on the table, but we nibble only with hesitation, never tasting its fullness. Healing begins when we can pause, notice the guilt, and ask: *"Who taught me that ease must be earned? Who told me that love is conditional?"* Slowly, the script can shift. Receiving becomes an act of courage, not entitlement, but trust. Trust that we are worthy of nourishment, joy, and kindness simply by being.

The truth is: bread doesn't ask to be earned. It only asks to be received.

15. The Inventory of My Worth

One day, I found myself sitting in a heavy *fog of despair*, wondering what I had really achieved in this life.

I was getting older.

No house of my own.

And a *nagging emptiness* that felt like it had been following me for years.

When despair swallowed me, I grabbed a pen—if I couldn't feel worthy, at least I could count on it.

So, I decided to do something simple: write down every accomplishment I could remember.

To my surprise, the list grew fast.

Certifications. Degrees. Skills.

Gardening. Cooking. Teaching. Coaching.

Fixing things around the house.

Spiritual practices.

Writing poetry and books.

Guiding people through their challenges.

Being a source of *inspiration*.

By the end, the page was full.

And I felt proud.

At first, it was a healthy pride, the kind that whispers, *"See, you've done something with your life."*

But somewhere along the way, the list stopped being just a reminder.

It became my *crown*.

When I married for the first time, my aunt told my ex-wife she was lucky to marry me.

The same words floated through the air in my second marriage.

And deep inside, I carried a thought I never said aloud: *"Can't you see how much I am worth? You should adore me."*

Sometimes, even now, that feeling slips back in, gently stroking my pride like an old friend who knows my weak spots.

And then God, in His mysterious mercy, has a way of bringing me back to the ground.

Both times, He took me to rock bottom and whispered:

"See? Without grace, you are nothing. Without humility, you are empty."

In those moments, I ask myself:

Will I surrender now?

Will I *finally put down this crown and just be*?

Sacred Pause and Reflections

- How much of your *self-esteem* depends on *achievements*, *roles*, or *external validation?*
- What happens inside you when those *external "crowns" are taken away?*
- Can you name one way you are *valuable simply because you exist*, without *needing to earn it?*

Psychological Lens

At its core, *The Inventory of My Worth* reflects a subtle but powerful ego defence: using *achievements as a shield.* Every certificate, promotion, or accomplishment becomes like a brick in a wall, separating oneself from others. On the surface, it looks like confidence: *"I've done so much; I've earned my place."* But underneath, it can slip into egoism, the quiet message to others being, *"You must prove yourself to reach me."*

In relationships, this dynamic can be particularly distancing. When one partner constantly raises the bar of their own worth, it unintentionally creates an imbalance: the other partner feels like they can't catch up, or that love itself must be earned. This is what attachment theorists call **conditional worth**, love tied not to presence, but to performance. Over time, the "list" becomes less a celebration of growth and more a wall that keeps intimacy at bay.

From a motivational psychology lens, each achievement here is **extrinsically fuelled**, not only by a desire to grow but also by the drive to prove. **Self-Worth Theory (Covington, 1992)** explains this as achievement-based self-esteem: "I matter because I achieve." Every success becomes fuel to silence an inner doubt; every failure, a threat to identity.

The paradox is clear: the very list that was meant to prove value ends up enslaving the self to endless proving. Instead of joy, each accomplishment becomes a stepping stone to the next, never quite enough, because the hunger beneath isn't for success but for acceptance.

Explained in relational terms, the list is less about what you've done and more about the message it carries: *"See me, value me, love me, but only if you can match me."* That is where the real wound lies.

16. The Boy Who Jumped

In my village, water was everywhere, life-giving, unpredictable, sometimes dangerous.

Just beyond our house stood an old temple, and behind it, a spring-fed reservoir where the whole village came to bathe.

It was deep, twenty feet, at least.

Deep enough to drown a boy who couldn't swim.

One day, my uncle stood on one corner of the reservoir while I lingered on the opposite side.

He called out, teasing, “Come on, jump in! I am right here.”

Before he finished the sentence, I leapt.

He wasn't ready.

I saw the worry flash in his eyes as he lunged forward.

Somehow, I made it out safely.

That wasn't the only time.

Another uncle, a retired army man, once walked with me along a small stream near our home during the monsoon season.

The current was fast, swollen, restless.

He asked, “What do you want to be when you grow up?”

“An army man,” I said without hesitation.

He chuckled. "Then you must be ready to jump into rivers."—before the last word left his mouth, I was already in the water.

The current grabbed me like a thief.

My uncle fought hard to pull me out.

I survived.

But something deeper was at play.

Looking back, I wonder, what was I really trying to prove?

I was just a boy.

No clear direction.

No inner anchor.

But desperate to show I was brave. Man enough. Worth something.

Maybe I wanted to prove it to my uncles.

Maybe to the village.

Or maybe… to my mother.

You see, I had a mole just above my belly button.

In village lore, it was a mark of low courage.

And I *believed* them.

So, I *jumped.*

Into *rivers.*

Into *danger.*

Into anything that might prove them *wrong.*

Sacred Pause and Reflections

- Can you recall a childhood moment when you wanted to take a *leap*, literal or *symbolic*, to *prove yourself?*
- The story also suggests that true *trust* isn't about seeing the whole path, but about believing you have *wings*. What does *"having wings"* mean to you?

Psychological Lens

At first glance, this is a story of a boy daring to leap where others hesitated. But underneath, it speaks to the psychology of **risk, courage,** and **identity formation**.

Developmental psychology reminds us that children grow their sense of self through trials. **Erik Erikson** described the stage of *industry vs. inferiority*: "Am I capable? Do I measure up to others?" The jump wasn't only physical; it was a test of worth and belonging.

And yet, courage doesn't grow in isolation. A friend's sister once shared with me a simple truth: when a child hides in a game of hide and seek, it matters when an adult validates them. "Yes, you're hidden, no one can find you." Or when a child tries something new, it matters to hear, "Yes, you did it." These moments, though small, become powerful imprints. They tell the child: *You are capable. You are seen.*

That day, my leap carried both forces: the inner fire of wanting to prove myself, and the silent longing for someone to affirm me. In fact, much of courage is this dance between **self-validation** and **external acknowledgement**. Social psychologists call it **social comparison**; we measure ourselves through the gaze of others. To hesitate meant possible shame; to jump meant dignity.

Neuropsychology shows us that fear and excitement are twins; the body trembles the same way in both states. The difference is in **cognitive appraisal**: how we interpret that rush. My leap was a reframing of fear into proof. It became my own small initiation ritual, much like cultural rites where young people cross thresholds of courage to be recognised as "more than before."

And the truth? It wasn't just the wall I jumped that day, it was the invisible wall of self-doubt. That wall still shows up later in life, in jobs, relationships, and choices. Each time, the boy who jumped whispers to me: *Leap again.*

In psychology, many acts of daring, especially in adolescence, carry a **double meaning**. On the surface, they look like testing courage or proving self-worth. But underneath, they can sometimes carry an unconscious whisper: “I am willing to risk it all, even life itself.”

This doesn't necessarily mean it was an outright suicidal impulse. Instead, it could be what existential psychology calls **flirting with annihilation**, the subconscious readiness to confront mortality, as if testing, “What if I don't make it?”

This dual voice, *“I am ready to jump”* and *“I am ready to die,”* is deeply human. Sometimes our courage is fuelled not only by the desire to live more fully, but also by an unspoken willingness to face death. In adolescence, this often shows up in risk behaviours (reckless driving, dares, dangerous stunts), which carry both the thrill of life and the shadow of *self-destruction.*

Symbolic Meaning

Symbolically, the boy’s jump is an archetypal **descent into the underworld**, a physical crossing into danger that mirrors a psychic plunge into the *shadow*. In myths, such acts often precede transformation, but only if the hero survives to integrate the experience. In Jungian terms, the jump could be seen as a confrontation with the *death instinct* (**Thanatos**), counterbalanced by the *survival instinct* (**Eros**) that ultimately pulls him back toward life.

The deeper takeaway: moments of extreme impulse are rarely about the leap itself, they are about what the person longs to escape, and the *unspoken hope that someone will notice* before they hit the ground.

17. Between Two Mothers

"I am going to see my mom today," my wife said casually over lunch, nibbling as she packed her bag.

"She's alone at home and my sister's going out, so I'll have dinner with her."

I nodded.

"Yeah, that's fine," I said.

My son's eyes lit up; he always loves going there. Truth be told, he rarely chooses to stay with me anyway—to avoid argument and confrontation.

After they left, the house fell quiet.

And in that silence… something stirred:

A flicker of *emptiness.*

A flicker of *resentment.*

And something else I couldn't name.

Later, while watching a healing video, a thought hit me like *a jolt of electricity:* it's my parents' 50th wedding anniversary this weekend.

Fifty years together. Half a century. And yet… we had not really talked about it. My wife had only asked once, lightly, if I'd like her to attend if I decided to go. I had shrugged it off at the time.

But now the contrast struck me.

Why did her mother's evening alone spark immediate action, while my parents' milestone felt like a passing cloud?

Why not for me?

Why not for them?

And the sharper question: *What kind of son am I?*

I could feel the guilt. Quiet. Heavy. Hiding beneath my breath.

Then another voice rose inside me, soft, steady:

Your mother lives her own karma. Her mother lives here.

Each is walking a path her soul agreed to long ago, reaping the fruits of choices, of prayers, of old wounds.

We often say astrologically that my mother is nearing *moksha*, that this life, with its aches, silences, and unmet expectations, may be her last. Maybe she's bearing it all so she never has to return.

So why the ache in me?

Why the lump in my throat?

Because I am still *human*.

Still a *son*.

Still, someone who wants to matter in the lives that matter to me.

I am still learning what it means to love without trying to fix it.

To honour without guilt.

To show up, even if it's just emotionally.

Maybe, like her, I too have a journey.

And maybe I, too, will keep returning, life after life, until I learn to love more purely… and let go more freely.

Sacred Pause and Reflections

- Have you ever felt *caught between two people you loved deeply*, afraid of *betraying one by choosing the other?*
- What memories come up when you think of *being nurtured* or when you *longed for nurture but didn't receive it fully?*

Psychological Lens

This story captures the tension of **role conflict**, when a person occupies multiple roles with competing demands and loyalties (**Kahn et al., 1964**). Here, I was emotionally and practically pulled between two central maternal figures, biological mother and mother-in-law, each carrying different emotional histories, expectations, and cultural meanings.

This dynamic often triggers **attachment-based conflicts**. The pull toward one's mother can activate **primary attachment bonds**, deep-seated needs for approval, care, and belonging. The pull toward the mother-in-law can be shaped by the partner relationship, the unspoken expectation to demonstrate loyalty to the spouse's family.

In such situations, there's also the presence of **triangulation (Bowen's Family Systems Theory),** when tension between two people is eased (or intensified) by involving a third. I may feel like a bridge between two worlds, yet also like a rope being pulled from both ends.

At a deeper level, guilt plays a central role here. **Survivor's guilt** in relationships can emerge when one feels they are neglecting one person's emotional needs to fulfil another's, even if both cannot be satisfied at once. This guilt is amplified in collectivist cultural contexts, where duty and family harmony are prized above personal comfort.

Symbolic Meaning

Symbolically, "two mothers" can be seen as **two archetypal forces (Jung)**, the mother as *Nurturer* and the mother as *Authority*. One might represent unconditional acceptance, the other conditional belonging. In myth and folklore, choosing between two maternal figures often mirrors the hero's choice between two paths, one rooted in the past, the other leading toward a new life stage.

The "space between" them is the symbolic **liminal zone**, a threshold space where identity is renegotiated. Living in this space is uncomfortable because it demands an ongoing balancing act without the relief of a final resolution.

The deeper truth is that the tension isn't about choosing one mother over the other, but about integrating these two inner archetypes, learning to honour loyalty without self-betrayal, and to love without carrying the impossible burden of satisfying everyone at once.

18. The Weight of Two Worlds

At 45, I am caught in a *storm.*

Not the kind with rain or thunder, this one brews in the silence between two questions:

Who am I to my mother?

Who am I to myself?

Every day, I perform a delicate dance.

To my mother, I wear the mask of a *man in motion*, faking calls, shaping hopeful stories, making it sound like I am one step away from something stable. Something worthy of her *worry.*

To my wife, I wear a different *silence.* She doesn't ask, doesn't press. Her stillness feels like support, and yet, sometimes, it feels like another *weight.* Not because she blames me, but because she *doesn't.*

And maybe… I crave *confrontation.* The mirror. The fire that would say:

"Yes, this burden is real. I see it too."

Some days, I don't know which side I belong to.

Do I lean into the guilt-ridden loyalty of a son chasing his mother's dreams?

Or drift into the quiet partnership where my worries live unspoken?

And then there's me, *trembling in the middle.*

Trying to balance the invisible scales of obligation and identity.

It doesn't feel like a midlife crisis.

It feels like erosion.

A slow wave washing away the roles I clung to, *provider, achiever, good son, spiritual seeker,* leaving questions I can no longer outrun.

My mind spins stories:

Maybe I am failing.

Maybe I am not man enough.

Maybe I am the only one stuck while the world moves forward.

But beneath that noise, a softer voice whispers:

This isn't failure.

I stood on the threshold, a liminal space.

It isn't about money, not entirely.

It's about *value*.

It's about where I place my *worth* when there's no resume to prove it.

It's about the *invisible contracts* we sign as sons, husbands, seekers, never noticing the fine print says: "*You must not disappoint.*"

What if growth means disappointing someone else to stay true to myself?

What if guilt isn't a curse, but a signal,

that I am leaving a cage?

I think of my wife's fierce loyalty to her family. I never questioned it.

Now I wonder: is my urge to be with my parent's pure *love*… or *penance?*

Am I trying to prove I am a *good son* so I don't feel like a *bad husband?*

Or am I just trapped, pulled by the quiet grief of not being enough for either?

The *triangle* haunts me only because I forgot,

I can step out.

I can stand in the middle and not be torn.

I can say:

"I am not a boy anymore. I am a man in transition. Please don't ask me to shrink into old shapes to comfort your fears."

Sacred Pause and Reflections

- Have you ever felt like you were living in two different *worlds*, each demanding a *different version* of you?
- What parts of yourself feel most *authentic*, and what parts feel shaped *by expectations of family, culture, or society?*
- How do you carry the *guilt or exhaustion* of trying to *please both worlds at once?*

Psychological Lens

This story reflects *role conflict,* the strain that comes from simultaneously inhabiting two or more roles with competing demands. I have been navigating the role of a *dutiful son* while also holding the role of a *partner in a marriage.*

From **Bowen's Family Systems Theory**, this is a clear case of **triangulation**, when an unresolved tension between two people (me and my mother) pulls in a third (my wife), creating a dynamic where my energy is divided and no relationship feels fully satisfied.

There's also a thread of **identity foreclosure**, a term from James Marcia's identity status theory, where a person adopts values and roles without fully exploring alternatives, often to please authority figures. I have long been guided by the "good son" contract without questioning whether that role aligns with my authentic self at this stage of life.

The moment of questioning, *"What if growth meant disappointing someone else to remain true to myself?"* is psychologically significant. It shows a shift from an **external locus of control** (worth tied to others' approval) toward an **internal locus of control** (worth tied to self-defined values). This is a classic **midlife individuation process**, as described by **Carl Jung**, moving from living for others to living from one's own centre.

Symbolic Meaning

The "two worlds" are not only the mother's expectations and the wife's quiet non-interference. They symbolise the world of *obligation* versus the world of *authenticity*. Standing between them places me in a *liminal space*, where loyalty and selfhood each demand acknowledgement.

The **invisible scales** represent *psychological equilibrium*, the inner balancing act between inherited duties (ancestral, cultural) and the soul's personal calling.

In mythic terms, this is the **Hero at the Crossroads** archetype. One path is the familiar road of filial loyalty, which promises belonging but often at the cost of autonomy. The other is the untrodden path of self-definition, which offers freedom but risks guilt and alienation.

The "quiet storm" reflects *psychic tension*, the inner turbulence that precedes conscious choice.

The key transformation hinted here is from **Son Consciousness** to **Self-Authoring Consciousness**, where I moved from being a caretaker of others' expectations to the author of my own life story.

19. Echoes of Worthiness

I had always been known for my leadership, sharp with patterns, tuned into team dynamics, and able to inspire results through insight rather than pressure.

I could see what others missed.

I could move people without forcing them.

That made me valuable.

I helped transform organisations, streamline processes, and spark momentum where there was none.

But 2013 cracked something open.

I wasn't just out of a job,

I was *let go*.

And for nine long months, I sat with that truth.

It became a strange kind of cocoon.

In the discomfort, something else began to grow.

I stepped onto the path of healing and coaching, becoming a past life regression therapist, a hypnotherapist, an agile coach.

Layer by layer, a new identity formed.

Then came 2019.

Another high point.

Another job lost, this time just before COVID.

Again, nine months without work.

The universe seemed to have me on a timer I didn't understand.

And in 2024, after moving to Vietnam and joining another MNC, it happened again.

Lost the job. Found another. I lost it in three months.

What was this rhythm I was caught in?

Then I saw it:

Every time I reached a peak, financially, professionally, something in me trembled.

A whisper: *"You're not worthy of this."*

Even when things were going well, unless the job challenged me to my core,

I would either sabotage it or feel the ground quietly slipping away.

I remembered all those years I had chanted for easy money, for abundance without effort.

And when it came, it felt *undeserved.*

Like I had tricked the system.

Like I had not *earned* it.

That's the thing about prayers: they get answered.

But they also expose the part of you that has not integrated the blessing.

One day, my son said something that stopped me cold: *"Shiroko (a character name) calls them (life events) echoes of indecision, where even thoughts can birth universes."*

Yes.

These echoes of mine,

the quiet *hesitations*,

the whispers of *unworthiness*, had been scripting my fate all along.

Sacred Pause and Reflections

- What is a *story from your life* where you felt you had to *prove your worth,* to yourself or to others?
- If the echoes of *unworthiness* could finally fade, what would the *truest voice of your worth* say to you now?
- What is one *small statement/action* you can *affirm your own worth* today, without needing any *external validation?*

Psychological Lens

This story brings me face-to-face with the deep, often unconscious dialogue between **self-worth and external validation**. The "echoes" here are not just sounds but the reverberations of old voices, parental, societal, and ancestral, that live inside and shape how I measure my value.

Psychologists describe this as **introjection**: when external judgments or expectations become internalised as our own self-talk. Over time, these voices no longer need to be spoken aloud; they replay inside us, shaping how we interpret our every success and failure.

In my case, I realised that praise or criticism from others didn't land on a blank slate; it landed on a pre-recorded echo chamber already filled with messages of *"you're enough"* or *"you're not enough."* When someone affirmed me, it resonated briefly, but when someone dismissed me, the echo grew louder, confirming a wound that was already there.

This is also where **conditional self-worth (Carl Rogers)** takes root. Instead of *"I am valuable because I exist,"* the inner contract becomes: *"I am valuable only if I perform, achieve, or meet expectations."* This conditionality breeds restlessness because no achievement ever silences the echoes fully; they just wait for the next moment of doubt to resurface.

Sometimes I wonder: was it my own voice doubting me, or was I still speaking with the voices of my parents, teachers, or bosses? This blurring of inner and outer voices is exactly what makes the echo so hard to escape.

Yet psychology also shows a way through: the practice of **self-compassion** (**Kristin Neff**). By learning to speak to oneself with the warmth one would offer a friend, the volume of the echoes begins to fade. Worthiness no longer has to be borrowed from others; it can be reclaimed from within.

Symbolic Meaning

The echo is more than a sound; It's a **mirror of the soul's unfinished dialogues**. An echo repeats what is spoken, but never originates on its own. In the same way, the worth I kept searching for outside was always a repetition of something I had not yet claimed inside.

Symbolically, the echo stands for the **gap between the self and the Self**, between the roles I perform and the essence that simply is. The echo will always return until I learn to stand in silence, rooted in my own presence.

True worthiness isn't proven through echoes. It's realised in stillness.

When the echoes no longer dictate my value, I can finally hear the quiet, steady voice of my authentic self: *"You were enough, all along."*

20. When the Roads Fell Silent

Spring, 2020: The world was slowing to a standstill, but inside me, panic was picking up speed.

Papa's urinary surgery had gone well in Gurgaon. We were only waiting for the final biopsy before heading home. I was at the office when Mummy called:

"The doctor wants you to come."

I thought it was for paperwork.

It wasn't.

The doctor's voice was calm, but his words burned:

"High-grade tumour in the bladder... You need to see a specialist."

From that moment, life became a loop of CT scans, radiotherapy sessions, waiting rooms, and hospital corridors.

And then, lockdown.

The city outside looked like an abandoned *film* set. Empty roads. Dry leaves scraping across cracked asphalt. As if the whole world had stopped to watch our *private battle.*

Inside, the three of us, me, Mummy, Papa, meditated, prayed, and practised energy healing. Papa's spirit burned like a torch in a dark tunnel. He even wrote a poem, gentle and luminous, that felt like medicine. Against all odds, radiotherapy worked. The report came back clean. We celebrated quietly.

For 2.5 years, the shadow stayed away.

Then it returned.

This time, I was in Vietnam. My sisters and brothers-in-law took charge, tests, consultations, and hospital visits. Papa researched late into the night, but his enthusiasm was dimmer now. Radiotherapy was no longer an option. Hormone therapy became the new path.

And me?

I carried a stone in my chest—*guilt*.

Guilt that I wasn't there in the waiting rooms.

Guilt that my absence might have made the fight lonelier this time.

I told myself, *He's still here. He's still fighting.*

But deep down, I feared something harder: that without my hand in his, the road ahead might feel *longer*.

Sacred Pause and Reflections

- Have you ever carried *guilt* for *not being there* for someone you love, whether by choice or by *circumstance*?
- How has the memory of your *father* shaped your *choices in life?*
- How can you begin to *release the guilt* and *transform it into a force for positive action* in your relationships today?

Psychological Lens

At its core, this story isn't just about illness; It's about the **psychological burden of guilt**. In psychology, **guilt** is understood as the emotional experience of believing one has violated a moral standard or let someone down (**Baumeister et al., 1994**). Unlike shame, which attacks the *self* ("I am bad"), guilt is tied to specific *behaviours or actions* ("I did something bad").

Here, the guilt emerges not from neglect or indifference, but from **physical absence**. You couldn't be present during your father's medical battle because of geographical and situational realities, yet the mind interprets absence as failure. This aligns with the concept of **survivor's guilt**, where one feels responsible for circumstances outside their control, often seen in caregiving or family crises.

Shame whispers: *"I am a bad son."*

Guilt whispers: *"I didn't do enough as a son."*

This is a form of **self-blame**, where we take on a responsibility that isn't ours, in an attempt to gain a sense of control over a situation we are powerless to change. The guilt becomes a way of staying connected to the pain, a misguided attempt to "share the burden" from afar.

Psychologists like **Brené Brown** highlight this critical difference: **shame corrodes the self**, while **guilt can motivate repair**. In this story, guilt doesn't come from apathy, but from **love**. It shows how deeply you wanted to be there, how tethered your identity as a son is to presence and care.

But what shame hides, rage often reveals. And when silence can no longer hold, fire erupts.

Chapter Four

The Fire of Unspoken Rage

"Anger is the bodyguard of pain."

21. The Frame and the Betrayal

Relationships are not transactions; there's a natural rhythm of giving and receiving, but once you start keeping score, you're no longer dancing together. You're running an accounting department.

After my first broken marriage, I wasn't searching for love. I was searching for *meaning*.

My father once told me, *"You've already built a frame in your mind and fixed a picture in it. That's why no one seems to fit."*

He was right. I had my *frame*, and I was simply waiting for the exact *picture* to match it.

Ironically, I found that picture in a spiritual retreat, even though my parents thought I should search on matrimonial sites, not meditation halls.

She was everything my "frame" wanted: a coach, a therapist, a trainer.
We got married. I moved to Vietnam.

We tried to build a life together, but the dream I'd imagined, the shared vision, never quite took shape.

One day, she said gently, *"You should build something new for yourself. don't depend on me."*

She was right. I didn't know the language. I couldn't socialise easily. She carried the weight of making things happen.

But in my mind, her words landed like betrayal.

We had come together to build *together*.

If I was meant to do it alone, why start at all?

And somewhere, a darker thought began to whisper: *If I succeed alone, it's all my work. and that I would have done it alone.*

I couldn't let go of the idea that I am together, and still, I have to do it *alone*.

That thought kept haunting me. Every time I take a step forward, this thought brings me two steps backwards. The thought of betrayal keeps banging at the back of my head and aches my heart.

It seeped into my mind, into my body, until all I could feel was the slow, heavy pull of *depression*.

Sacred Pause and Reflections

- Have you ever realised that someone you saw as an *enemy* or a *competitor* was actually a *teacher* or a *mirror*?
- Can you recall a moment when someone's words/actions hurt you, but later you realised it was your *interpretation* that *magnified the pain?*
- What would it look like to build a new *"frame"* together with someone, instead of waiting for them to *fit into yours?*

Psychological Lens

This story isn't just about a frame or even about betrayal in the literal sense. It's about the invisible contracts we carry inside relationships, the unspoken expectations of loyalty, recognition, and fairness, and what happens when those contracts are broken. The frame becomes more than an object; it becomes a symbol of shattered trust.

Psychologically, betrayal cuts deep because it destabilises two things at once: our sense of safety in the other person, and our sense of coherence in ourselves. **Attachment theory** tells us that trust is the foundation of secure bonds. When betrayal enters, it doesn't just feel like losing another person's loyalty; it feels like losing the ground beneath us. It threatens what John Bowlby called our *secure base*.

There is also the experience of **betrayal trauma (Freyd, 1996)**, the unique wound caused when the very person we rely on for safety becomes the source of harm. This kind of rupture creates a painful double bind: we want to cling to the bond for survival, yet we also recoil from it in self-protection. That inner push-pull is often more exhausting than the betrayal itself.

The protagonist's subsequent obsession with the thought of betrayal is a classic example of **rumination**. The mind circles endlessly, trying to reconcile two opposing realities: "I trusted you" and "you hurt me." This unresolved conflict becomes a breeding ground for emotional pain and, as the story reveals, leads to a state of emotional paralysis and depression. The betrayal lives on not only in the event but in the mind's inability to let it settle.

In many cases, betrayal activates **schemas of abandonment and mistrust (Young, Schema Therapy**). The mind replays: *"I cannot rely on anyone... I am foolish to trust... I am unsafe in closeness."* And yet, paradoxically, betrayal can also awaken our deepest longing for authentic connection, because only when something cracks do we see how much we were depending on it.

The true work of healing isn't about finding someone who fits our pre-existing "frame," but about dismantling the frame itself. Healing means loosening our grip on rigid expectations so that relationships can be more authentic, co-created, and resilient. The broken frame becomes a mirror, reflecting both the fragility of our trust and the possibility of rebuilding it with new strength.

In another lens: What first appeared as betrayal can also be understood as part of a deeper unconscious contract within the relationship, a mirror set up not to break me, but to grow me. By withdrawing, my partner forced me to confront the belief that I could only create with support.

Psychologically, this shift aligns with Jung's idea of individuation, where the Self emerges when external scaffolding falls away. The "frame" of betrayal wasn't just about abandonment; it was also a silent initiation, saying: *if you can build even when left alone, then the opportunity has already arrived in you.* In this light, the betrayal becomes less a wound and more a mirror, reflecting the strength and creativity that were waiting to be claimed.

22. The Real Cost of Anger

Last night, I asked my wife to sleep early.

She had a training session the next morning, and I wanted her to rest.

I said it gently, but inside, something was *tightening*.

She kept scrolling, searching for more examples to prepare for her class.

My chest felt warm with irritation, like pressure building behind a closed door.

I didn't say anything. Not at first.

But the anger was there.

And the strange part was… I'd been here before.

Just a few nights earlier, she had brought up the same training content late at night. That time I snapped:

"*Why do you always come at the last minute? Why work yourself into anxiety and then lose sleep over it?*"

Now, the same storm was building.

My body ached with tension.

My breath had turned shallow.

My mind was trying to focus on a psychotherapy book, but my soul felt like it needed therapy.

Why do I get so angry about this?

Why does my nervous system go into battle mode when she's simply preparing for something she cares about?

And then, unexpectedly, the truth surfaced.

It wasn't about her content being late.

It wasn't even about *"the sleep"*.

It was about *sickness.*

If she didn't rest, she might fall ill.

If she fell ill, we might need a hospital.

Hospitals mean money.

Money! What—!!!

The anger wasn't really about her at all.

It was about me, my fear, my insecurity, my quiet panic over finances I rarely speak of.

My rage wasn't anything more than a bodyguard, protecting a deeply buried fear: *What if we don't have enough?*

And in that moment, everything clicked.

I often tell myself I've changed, that I've evolved past the money anxieties that once haunted me.

But maybe the universe was just waiting for the right moment, the right trigger, to show me what still needed healing.

Last night, it did.

Sacred Pause and Reflections

- When was the last time you felt *angry* at someone or something?
- What is the *REAL* equation of your own *anger*?
- What is a story from your life where anger served as a *protector*? What *boundary was being crossed?*
- Can you think of a time when you used *anger as a mask to hide* a more *vulnerable feeling,* like *sadness or fear?*

Psychological Lens

Anger sometimes arrived like a storm, *loud, hot, and convincing.* In the moment you can feel so real, so justified, that you will rarely stop to ask: *what lies beneath this fire?*

In therapy, we can understand that anger can be a s**econdary emotion**, a shield that covers something more vulnerable.

Primary emotions are raw, immediate, and closer to the core. Fear when you hear a sudden noise in the night. Sadness when someone you love walks away. Joy when a child smiles at you. These arise directly from the experience itself. They are unfiltered, honest responses of the heart and body.

Secondary emotions, on the other hand, are layered on top of those primary states, often as a defence. Sometimes anger is easier to express, safer to display, than saying out loud: *I am hurt.*

I remember someone sharing that whenever his needs were ignored, the very first wave inside him wasn't anger at all, it was sadness. A simple, raw ache that whispered, *"You don't matter."* But sadness felt too soft, too powerless to carry. Almost instantly, it transformed into anger. Anger gave him something sadness couldn't: force, fire, a sense of control. Yet every time anger took the stage, the sadness was pushed back into silence, left unresolved,

n therapy, I came to see another truth: anger **isn't** just an emotion—it's also a *resource drain.* Holding it, expressing it, and recovering from it takes enormous energy. It tenses the body, floods the nervous system, and leaves behind exhaustion.

The more I lived in anger, the less I had left for healing, for connection, for creativity.

The real cost of anger, then, wasn't only in the words we said or the relationships we strained. The cost was also inside us, the way anger consumed the energy we could have used to feel, to grieve, to *love*.

23. The Podcast That Poked My Wound

Today, I was listening to a podcast, one of those *polished, slightly self-congratulatory* ones about relationships, soulmates, and marriage.

The hosts, both counsellors, were talking about "values."

But then one of them listed *career as a value*… without tying it to anything deeper.

Something in me tightened.

Every few minutes, they slipped in a line:

"In our workshop, we go deeper into this."

"We work on this live with couples."

A familiar heat started to rise in my chest.

Then came the sharper edge: rage.

How can they misguide people like this?

How can they turn sacred work into a marketing tactic?

But then… I stopped.

I asked myself the uncomfortable question:

Why is this bothering me so much?

And under the righteous anger, I found something softer. Sadder. Truer.

It wasn't really about them.

It was about me.

I have not done a podcast yet.

I have not claimed that platform.

I have not been invited to share my truth.

I've been waiting, quietly, invisibly, while others speak loudly.

And part of me feels… left behind.

The anger wasn't about their voice.

It was about my *silence.*

But now that I see it, I won't let it curdle into bitterness.

I'll let it become a call to action.

I will build my voice.

Not to compete, but to contribute.

Not to correct them, but to connect with those who are still waiting to hear *my truth.*

Sacred Pause and Reflections

- When was the last time something *seemingly ordinary*—a podcast, a song, a conversation—touched a *wound you thought had healed?*
- If yes, how did you respond at that moment? Did you *turn away*, or did you *lean into it?*
- What is your "My truth" at that moment?

Psychological Lens

This story is less about the podcast itself and more about what it awakened inside me. Psychologists call this an **emotional trigger**, an external cue that reactivates unresolved wounds or unprocessed experiences. The podcast didn't create my pain; it simply *activated* it, much like how a familiar smell, song, or phrase can transport us back to a place we thought we had long left behind.

And then there was jealousy. Not the sharp, envious kind, but the quieter ache of *"why not me?"* In psychology, jealousy is often described as a **secondary emotion**, a mask over more tender truths like fear of being left behind, insecurity about self-worth, or longing for recognition. On the surface, it looks like I resented the other person's success; underneath, I was grieving the parts of me that still doubted whether I deserved the same.

Jealousy in that moment became a mirror. Not a mirror of the podcaster, but of myself. It reflected both the confidence I admired and the silence I carried inside. What I thought I lacked in myself shone brighter in the other, which is why it stung so deeply.

Here, the **Seven Essene Mirrors** offer another lens. They teach us that what we encounter in others is often a reflection of something unresolved within ourselves. Sometimes people mirror back what we judge, sometimes what we've lost, sometimes what we are ready to grow into. In this case, the podcast host became a mirror of my unexpressed confidence and my unclaimed voice. What I admired in them was also a signpost toward the parts of myself I had silenced.

The podcast became more than background noise. It became a mirror, not of the world outside, but of the inner fragments waiting for recognition. It didn't just give me information; it exposed the fragile places inside me that were waiting to be acknowledged, not avoided.

Symbolic Meaning

The podcast is the modern equivalent of an oracle, speaking words that pierce straight through to a tender spot. It reminds us that we don't always control when the wound gets touched, but we do control whether we use that moment as a cue to defend or a cue to heal. In Jungian symbolism, the "voice in the air" becomes the archetypal *Herald*, the figure that calls the hero to face an inner journey they've been avoiding.

24. The Helplessness Beneath the Rage

In the 1980s, American Airlines, under Robert L. Crandall's leadership, made a decision that became legendary: Remove a single olive from every first-class salad.

Savings? Forty thousand dollars a year.

I was fascinated.

One small, thoughtful decision, massive impact.

That, to me, was *leadership*. That was *vision*.

I wanted to make decisions like that in my own life, decisions that mattered, that made a difference.

But life had other plans.

Life tested me, and tested me again, until something inside began to *crack*.

The very examples that once inspired me began to… rot.

I didn't quite become the leader I imagined.

Not the *successful son.*

Not the *perfect husband.*

Not the *ideal father*.

I started noticing other "brilliant" corporate moves, only now, they didn't look clever.

They looked manipulative.

Toothpaste companies are widening tube openings so you squeeze out more, using it up faster, buying it sooner.

Shampoo brands drying out your hair just enough that you'll "need" their conditioner… and then their serum… and then their vitamins.

Fashion brands staging "limited stock" signs to make you panic-buy.

And then there were the subtle mimic manipulations, ads that didn't just sell products, but imitated human connection so well you forgot it was scripted.

A fake laugh.

A well-timed pause.

A hand on the heart, like they really cared.

One day, a friend told me she didn't own a fan.

"Fans are low status," she said casually. "You have to have AC; it's a status symbol."

I stared at her, heat rising in my chest.

These companies were not just selling products; they were selling stories.

Stories that rewrote our values while we were not looking.

And I had been buying them.

We all had.

The realisation burned.

I got angry.

So angry, I stopped using toothpaste altogether, my tiny rebellion.
I refused to buy "status" air-conditioning and stuck to a fan.

But then I noticed something. The anger was only a mask.

Beneath it was *helplessness*.

I felt helpless that I couldn't stop the machine.

Helplessness that no matter how much I rebelled, the stories were still shaping the world around me.

And slowly, that helplessness turned into reflection.

If I couldn't control the world, perhaps I could at least control myself.
Instead of raging against manipulation, I began asking: *How can I reflect values like integrity, simplicity, and respect, without imposing them on others?*

That became my quiet practice.

Not forcing, not preaching.

Just embodying.

The bigger question shifted from "Why don't they live by these values?" to "How can I live them without needing anyone else's approval?"

In that shift, the helplessness *softened.*

The rage *dissolved.*

And what remained was a different kind of leadership, one not about olives or marketing tricks, but about living one's values without making them a weapon.

Sacred Pause and Reflections

- Do you ever find yourself *dismissing or criticising others* as a way of protecting yourself from feeling *"less than"*?
- Can you recall a time when someone you admired suddenly *stirred resentment or envy* in you? What was *beneath that shift?*

Psychological Lens

At first glance, this story looks like anger at consumer manipulation, but psychologically, it reveals a deeper process. What appears as rage is often a **secondary emotion**, a surface reaction that hides something more vulnerable underneath. Beneath the anger here lies **helplessness**, a primary emotion born from the recognition that one cannot fully control the forces shaping culture, markets, or even loved ones' values.

This movement from inspiration (*the olive story*) to disillusionment (*corporate tricks*) is also a case of **affective transference**. The admiration I once carried for bold leadership decisions became projected onto corporations, only later to swing into betrayal when those same systems proved manipulative. The anger was less about toothpaste tubes or ACs and more about a broken relationship with the very idea of leadership.

Psychologically, this is a shift from **idealisation to devaluation**, a common defence mechanism when our heroes fall from the pedestal, we place them on. First, they are larger than life; then, when disillusionment sets in, they become villains. But in both extremes, the real inner task is avoided: holding complexity.

The helplessness that follows reveals a turning point. Instead of remaining trapped in rage or cynicism, the story pivots toward **value integration**. In therapy, this would be seen as moving from an external locus of control (blaming systems) toward an internal locus of control (embodying values without imposing them). This shift mirrors what **Viktor Frankl** described as *freedom of attitude*: even when we cannot control the external, we retain the freedom to decide how we respond.

In this sense, the story isn't about rage at all. It's about learning how to metabolise helplessness into reflection, and how leadership can be redefined not as controlling systems or people, but as quietly embodying the values one wishes to see.

25. The Exit Before the Ascent

My first job was at Maruti Private India Ltd. in Gurgaon, still one of the richest learning experiences of my life.

I worked alongside a senior colleague on a project involving radio frequency terminals, complex, fascinating, and way ahead of its time for me.

Then the senior colleague had to leave.

My mentor turned to me and asked, "Can you take this on alone?"

I hesitated, then said yes.

The hurdles were real, but I managed to complete the project solo.
That success felt good, like proof I could handle more.

Soon after, I landed a job at a multinational company, a big deal back then because MNC culture was new to everyone.

When I resigned from Maruti, my super boss pulled me in.

He told me they'd been planning a major opportunity for me: to lead a project in a new plant nearby.

"Stay," he said. "Big things are coming."

I didn't stay in Maruti.

At the MNC, things moved quickly. I was soon sent to Dubai to handle a critical project.

It went well, another high. Everything seemed to be aligning.

And then… about a year and a half later, I took another job offer in Gurgaon.

Only after resigning did I learn the company had been planning to make me their point person for Dubai operations, a huge leadership role.

Again, I walked away.

Not once, but twice.

I was great at execution.

Great at solving problems.

Great at delivering results.

But every time I stood at the edge of a breakthrough, every time real leadership was about to begin, I left.

I told myself I was chasing better jobs.

The truth?

I was running from bigger responsibilities.

a hidden pattern that needs to be resolved before I move ahead in taking a bigger leadership role.

Sacred Pause and Reflections

- Have you ever found yourself *quitting, delaying, or pulling back* just when *something important was about to happen?*
- Does part of you believe you are *undeserving*, that if *you rise higher,* people will *"find you out"*?

Psychological Lens

On the surface, these are just career moves: one company to another, one opportunity traded for the promise of something bigger. But beneath the surface lies a deeper psychological pattern: the rhythm of ascent and retreat.

This story is an example of *fear of success* (sometimes called success anxiety). It isn't fear of failure, because I have proven again and again that I could deliver results. The fear was of what came *after success*: the weight of visibility, the expectation of sustaining it, the identity shift that true leadership demands.

Psychologists often describe this as *self-sabotage*: when opportunities align, some part of the psyche unconsciously *withdraws*. It isn't laziness, nor lack of ability, but rather an internal conflict between the part of me that longs to grow, and the part of me terrified of what growth will cost. In my case, the pattern was clear: each time I reached the doorway of leadership, I found a reason to walk away.

From a developmental lens, this reveals an underlying *avoidant coping style*. Avoidance is one of the most common defence mechanisms when our inner world feels unprepared for outer expectations. It's easier to change jobs (an external exit) than to confront the anxiety of responsibility (an internal ascent).

This also connects with **unfinished gestalt**, cycles of growth that begin but never complete. Each incomplete ascent left behind a residue of "what if," a subtle guilt that I carried into the next chapter. Over time, these residues accumulate, shaping a narrative not of capability, but of hesitation.

Another psychological layer here is *ego protection*. Taking on bigger roles meant confronting the risk of exposure, the possibility that I might not live up to the promise others saw in me. By exiting early, I kept my self-image safe. The paradox is cruel: in protecting the ego from potential failure, I denied myself the chance of fuller expansion.

Yet, these exits were not wasted. In therapy, we sometimes reframe such patterns as *rehearsals for readiness*. Every cycle of ascent and retreat is part of the soul's way of preparing itself. The exits themselves carry lessons about responsibility, about fear, about identity.

The real healing begins when we stop judging the exits as mistakes and begin to ask: *What part of me was afraid to rise? And what would it take for me to stay this time?*

Symbolic Meaning

Symbolically, this is the **mountain path left halfway,** the traveller turns back not because the road is blocked, but because the summit feels too bright to stand in. In mythic terms, It's the *"refusal of the return"* from **Joseph Campbell's Hero's Journey**, the point where the hero resists bringing home the gift because doing so requires full transformation (lost old identity). The lesson here: the climb is rarely as dangerous as the *story we tell ourselves about what awaits at the top.*

26. From Pedestals to Ground Level

Being the youngest in the family meant I never had to ask for love; it was already there, wrapped around me like a soft blanket.

My plate was always full.

My clothes were always ironed.

My school fees were paid without hesitation.

In that warmth, I thrived.

At school, I was the class monitor, the teachers counted on; My name was called for competitions, my photo pinned to the notice boards.

In college, it was no different: debates, declamations, cultural events. I had a place in the spotlight, and I wore it like a *second skin.*

When I landed a job in a multinational company, my family's pride lit up the room.

"Our son is in a big company now," they said.

It felt like the pedestal had only grown taller.

Until I stepped into the office in a new city.

There, I was no one.

The junior. The newcomer.

My medals meant nothing. My applause had expired.

The fall was quiet, but sharp.

From years of being "somebody," I was now starting from zero.

And no mother was waiting at home with food.

No family asking how my day went.

No daily reminder that I was already loved, already enough.

I still remember a senior saying, "Why are you leaving so early? People who leave early don't get good appraisals. Those who stay late do."

It wasn't advice, it was a rule.

And this was a world where perception outweighed truth.

So, I stayed late when needed. I learned the unspoken codes. I built my image from scratch, brick by brick.

But sometimes, late at night at work, I think of those earlier years in school,

when love didn't have to be earned,

and worth wasn't something I had to prove.

Sacred Pause and Reflections

- Have you ever been placed on a *pedestal* by others? How did it feel to carry that *expectation*?
- When you step from the *familiar* into the *unknown*, which feeling greets you first—*fear, curiosity, or freedom?*

Psychological Lens

Putting someone on a pedestal feels like admiration, but in truth, it's a subtle act of *distortion.* When I lifted certain teachers, mentors, or partners above me, I wasn't only seeing their brilliance, but I was also *shrinking myself.* Psychologists describe this dynamic as **idealisation (Sigmund Freud, 1914)**, a defence mechanism where we exaggerate another person's qualities to create safety, direction, or even a sense of identity. In psychodynamic theory, it often comes hand in hand with **devaluation (Otto Kernberg)**, because once the illusion cracks, disappointment floods in, and the fall from the pedestal can feel violent, both for them and for me.

What sat underneath my pedestal-building wasn't just admiration, it was **self-doubt**. It was easier to project wisdom, strength, or authority onto another than to own the possibility that I carried those qualities too. **Carl Rogers (1959)** might call this living under **conditions of worth**, the belief that I am only valuable when someone greater than me validates my existence. By raising them higher, I avoided confronting my own insecurities.

And yet, the moment of bringing them back down to ground level was equally revealing. It was never really about them. It was about my own relationship with *equality*, with recognising that the people I glorify are human, just as I am. That their flaws don't erase their worth, and my flaws don't erase mine.

In therapy, this kind of work is called **deconstructing projections (Carl Jung, 1946)**. It's less about tearing others down and more about integrating the qualities we admire (or despise) into ourselves. The "ground level" isn't a loss of respect; It's a gain of wholeness. It's the realisation that growth comes not from worshipping another's light, but from recognising that *same light within.*

Symbolic Meaning

Symbolically, the pedestal represents **hierarchical spirituality**, where wisdom is believed to flow only from the "higher" to the "lower." Stepping down from the pedestal (or bringing someone down from it) is akin to reclaiming **horizontal connection**, where truth is exchanged openly without authority as a filter.

The ground level in the story symbolises **humility and mutual recognition**. It's the fertile soil where authentic relationships can grow, free from distortion caused by worship or projection.

The deeper insight: in spiritual and personal growth, the moment we stop needing to be above or below someone else, we step into the only true space for *transformation*, eye to eye, heart to heart.

27. The Balloon

"Let's go for coffee today," my wife said, her eyes warm, the kind of look that already assumes my answer will be yes.

I smiled and reached for my wallet. She, in turn, began rummaging through her purse, pulling out scraps, receipts, and things she had not touched in months. It struck me how often we carry things we no longer need, letting them pile up until they become a quiet burden. Sometimes, I thought, we do the same with our emotions, dragging them along through the years, hoping someone will come and help lighten the load.

We found ourselves in a quiet coffee shop by the river. The air was still, the water moving lazily as if it had nowhere else to go.

Breaking the silence, my wife began talking about her elder sister.
"She's so happy today," she said. "She's going to Thailand for a retreat. Her husband finally agreed to let her go. They even fought about it yesterday."

I could see the sparkle in her eyes; she was genuinely happy for her sister. But beneath her words, there was a *shadow*.

Her sister has breast cancer. Just yesterday, she had felt that her husband wasn't taking good enough care of her. And yet, here they were, sending her off to Thailand.

I smiled faintly into my cup, not from amusement but from something else. My wife caught the smile and tilted her head, curious.

Memories were stirring. On our last trip together, I had jokingly asked my brother-in-law how he managed to travel with over

100 kilos of luggage every single time. He had smiled, but there was a quiet heaviness behind it.

"After a while," he said softly, *"when things no longer matter... You just let them be."*

Everyone in the family knew that whenever my sister-in-law travelled, she had to pay extra baggage fees at the airport. My brother-in-law had stopped trying to change that.

And I thought, was this quiet acceptance a sign of his love? Was letting her go to Thailand also an act of the same love?

My thoughts circled back to my own life. Was I, too, accepting small burdens in silence, letting them pile up in the name of love?

I remembered the last time I tried opening my heart to my wife. She had encouraged me to think positively. She meant well, but she didn't realise, I wasn't looking for a motivational push. I wasn't searching for silver linings. I wanted her to see my pain, to sit with me in it, the way one sits quietly on the bank of a flowing river, not to change the current but to *witness it.*

Moments like these, small but unresolved, feel like air filling a *balloon*. No one knows when it might burst.

"What are you thinking?" Her voice pulled me back.

Before I could answer, she asked, "You know what a sphinx is?"

I shook my head. "No."

"You don't even know that? Oh my God," she laughed, holding her hand up to her ear like a phone.

I looked at her, half-smiling, and said quietly, *"You just blew one more breath into the balloon."*

"Blow? Balloon?" she repeated, puzzled, as I sipped my coffee, letting the *river outside answer for me.*

Sacred Pause and Reflections

- Do you tend to hold on *tightly* in life, or do you find it easier to let things *drift away*?
- What does *"the gentle act of releasing"* look like for you, and what kind of freedom do you believe is waiting for you on the other side?

Psychological Lens

On the surface, this story is about a coffee outing and casual conversation. Psychologically, it illustrates *projection*, *attachment*, and *emotional containment*. My irritation at my wife's happiness isn't about her; it reflects my own unresolved tension around letting go, accepting impermanence, and sitting with discomfort.

The balloon became a symbol of my *unspoken needs, accumulated emotions, and relational patterns* I had carried for years. I realised I was **projecting**: imagining she sought importance or had forgotten me, not because she did, but because I had once felt *unseen*, *powerless*, and *overlooked*.

In **attachment theory (Bowlby)**, we often carry emotional "balloons", roles, relationships, identities, or expectations, not because they are still functional, but because they once gave us comfort or validation.

Letting go is frightening due to **loss aversion (Kahneman & Tversky)**: the anticipated pain of losing something outweighs the potential joy of what could replace it. I could feel the parts of me in tension: the *wounded self* - longing for recognition, the *supportive self* - wanting to celebrate her joy, and the *observing self* quietly noticing the dynamics at play.

Holding the balloon too tightly can lead to **enmeshment**, where our sense of self-worth is tied entirely to its presence. The anxiety about letting it go can also reflect *object permanence* wounds from early childhood, the fear that once something is out of sight, it's gone forever, along with the security it brought.

The *"string"* is psychologically important. It represents the thin, fragile connection between self and object of attachment, a symbol of hope, control, and the illusion that we can preserve something by holding on "just a little longer." I notice my mind assigning meaning to my wife's actions. **Projection** plays a role; I imagine she seeks importance or is careless, not because she is, but because I once felt unseen or powerless. These **micro dynamics** illuminate how past relational experiences shadow present intimacy and how subtle cues can trigger *unresolved feelings*.

The balloon also reflects emotional regulation and containment. Unacknowledged emotions expand internally until they find expression, through shared conversation or silent observation. Naming it, acknowledging the balloon, becomes a form of psychological self-soothing and mindful witness, transforming potential tension into awareness.

In marital dynamics, each unacknowledged hurt or dismissive comment adds another breath of air. What looks like silence is actually *accumulation*, and failing to release the pressure risks ruptures that feel sudden but have been quietly building for years.

Symbolic Meaning

In symbolism, a balloon represents *lightness*, *dreams*, and *childlike wonder*, but it's also fragile and temporary. The higher it floats, the more distance it creates between where we are and where it's heading.

The act of releasing a balloon can be seen as a **ritual of surrender**—acknowledging that some things are meant to rise beyond our reach. The balloon's upward journey symbolizes liberation, but also the grief of accepting impermanence.

In many spiritual traditions, the balloon's release is akin to letting go of karma, expectations, or control over outcomes. In Eastern spiritual traditions, this echoes the practice of *non-attachment* (vairāgya in yoga philosophy). To hold a balloon loosely is to enjoy its beauty without demanding permanence. In Buddhist thought, clinging creates *suffering*, while release brings *freedom*. It's a reminder that joy and beauty are sometimes meant to be experienced without ownership.

The balloon teaches that joy, like *breath itself*, is only ever borrowed.

Ultimately, the balloon teaches that not every loss is a tragedy; some are *invitations to expand* into a space where our hands are free for what's next.

28. The Alchemy of Emotions

One morning, my phone lit up with a call from an old friend in the U.S., well-settled now, doing great by all *outward signs*.

I glanced at it and thought, *Ah... another manifestation request?*

We used to work together. He was a relentless hustler, juggling multiple jobs, chasing every opportunity. His wife, equally devoted, anchored her hope in rituals and fasts for the goddesses, offering prayers for prosperity. I rented a small place near there, and over the years, it became part of my emotional world.

There's one night I'll never forget.

His wife called in panic; he'd gone missing. She feared the worst… maybe he'd jumped in front of a metro train.

I dropped everything. Searched for hours. Found him. Alive. Shaken. And I handed him back to her the way you return a child to a mother, carefully, reverently, *completely drained.*

Years later, he told me something I didn't expect.

"You know… whatever you used to say always came true. That's why I kept coming to you, for *confirmation*. You had that gift."

He eventually left for the U.S., and life opened up for him in ways I once *dreamed for myself.* I, meanwhile, walked my own *winters*, different struggles, different storms.

Even now, when his name flashes on my phone, something stirs.

A tightness. A resistance.

A voice that says:

Oh, now you remember me? Now, when you've made it?

And that's when I caught myself.

Not just as a friend.

But as a *psychologist*.

As a man who has spent 25 years watching how the human heart holds *contradictions*.

This feeling, the quiet envy, the faint resentment, isn't just about him. It's about me.

For years, I had unknowingly projected my own unlived potential onto him. He was the one I *"helped,"* the one who *"listened"* and *"acted."* In some way, I made him the carrier of my dreams. His wins became proof of my insight. And somewhere inside, I expected that when he rose, I'd rise with him, or at least be acknowledged for my *invisible role* in his story.

When that recognition never came, the *idealisation cracked…* and what came out was *raw, unfiltered.*

On the other side:

I *should* be happy for him.

I *want* to be happy for him.

And yet… I am not. Not entirely.

That's when shame creeps in, the kind that whispers:

"You're not as noble as you think."

"You're not a good friend."

But *I've learned to sit with shame. Not fight it. Not dress it up.* Because beneath every morally uncomfortable emotion lies a deeper truth.

It wasn't about his success.

It wasn't even about our friendship.

It was about my own *grief.*

The *grief of not yet becoming* who I wanted to be.

The grief of giving pieces of myself to others and hoping they'd carry them with *reverence.*

And the painful realisation that no one, not even those you've saved, *owes you anything.*

One part of me needed external validation to feel powerful.

One part that only felt valuable when someone came to me for answers.

And one part believed proximity to someone else's success could heal my *own wounds.*

Only then can it be the *emotional shift.*

Not by suppressing it.

But by alchemising it, with *honesty, humility, and healing.*

This isn't a story about being *bad* or *being jealous.*

It's a story about being a *fully feeling one.*

And that, too, is part of the *work.*

Sacred Pause and Reflections

- Have you ever carried *quiet resentment* or envy when someone you once supported seemed to *"forget"* your role in their journey? What emotions *surfaced* for you at that moment?
- In what ways have you, consciously or unconsciously, *projected your own unlived dreams or desires* onto others, hoping their success might also *validate your worth*?
- When you notice yourself seeking *recognition* or *validation* from others, how might you begin to *turn that longing inward to honour your own worth*, independent of *external acknowledgement*?

Psychological Lens

This story illustrates the process of **emotional transmutation**, turning raw, potentially destructive emotions into self-awareness and insight. In psychology, these mirrors **affect labelling (Lieberman et al., 2007)**, where simply naming an emotion can reduce its intensity and allow for better regulation.

My journey reflects **emotional alchemy**, a concept drawn from both Jungian psychology and mindfulness practice, taking the "base metals" of anger, jealousy, or fear and transforming them into "gold" through *conscious processing*.

The emotions themselves are not the problem; it's the **identification** with them that causes suffering. By stepping back into the observer role, I began to shift from **emotional fusion** (being consumed by feelings) to **emotional differentiation** (holding them without being defined by them).

From a **psychodynamic** perspective, the process also engages **shadow integration (Jung)**. Emotions we judge as "unspiritual" or "negative" are often exiled into the unconscious.

Bringing them into awareness without judgment allows for *wholeness*, reducing the inner split between the *"ideal self"* and the *"emotional self."*

Symbolic Meaning

Alchemy here isn't just a metaphor for change; it's a symbolic journey. In traditional alchemy, transformation involves three core stages: **nigredo** (blackening, the breakdown), **albedo** (whitening, purification), and **rubedo** (reddening, integration and creation).

In the story, the raw surge of difficult feelings represents **nigredo**, the chaotic stage where old identities and defences dissolve. The act of observing the emotion, naming it, and allowing it space reflects **albedo**, the purification through conscious awareness. Finally, the insight that emerges, that emotions are not enemies but messengers, is **rubedo**, the creation of a *new, integrated way of being.*

Symbolically, this is the **Magician archetype** in action, not in the sense of controlling life's events, but in learning to transform inner lead into gold. The *"alchemy"* isn't about removing discomfort, but about using it as the *fire that forges a more whole self.*

29. It is Good to Be Bad

When my first marriage broke up, the shock wasn't mine alone; *it rippled through every person* who thought they knew me.

"How can this be? Ankur? The one who helps people navigate relationships? The wise one? The man who gives guidance to so many couldn't make his own marriage work?"

Their disbelief echoed in my own chest. I could see the unspoken verdict in their eyes: *You were supposed to know better.*

Then came my first job loss.

Not my choice. Not my plan.

I'd taken the job under someone else's influence, and my parents looked at me as if I'd thrown away my future.

"How can a so-called smart person let go of the job he manifested... just like that?"

It happened again and again, moments where people expected me to rise, to be right, to be wise.

And each time I faltered, the weight of their *expectations pressed harder* on my chest.

Why did I have to keep living up to them?

Because I was obedient.

Because I was organised.

Because I was "the good one."

I wanted to stay in everyone's good books.

I wanted appreciation.

I wanted the nods of approval, the *"That's our Ankur."*

But one question began to drill into my mind:

Why can't I be wrong? Why can't I be "bad" and still make good decisions?

Then I watched *Raavan (The Movie).*

In it, the villain is unapologetically bad.

Nobody expects him to be virtuous, so he's free.

No *expectations.*

No *image* to protect.

No *pedestal* to balance on.

That's when a *dangerous, liberating* thought took root: Sometimes, it's good to be bad.

Not cruel. Not destructive. Just *free from the prison of perfection.*

Sacred Pause and Reflections

- Where in your life do you feel pressured to be *"good," even when it hurts you?*
- Where in your life are you still playing the role of *"the good one"* to meet others' *expectations*?
- Whose approval are you silently *living for*?

Psychological Lens

This story isn't about celebrating cruelty or glorifying rebellion. It's about the invisible weight of always being the "good one." The pleaser, the responsible one, the wise one. What sounds virtuous on the outside often becomes suffocating on the inside. Sometimes the greatest act of self-care is daring to step out of that costume, even if only for a moment, and reclaiming freedom from others' expectations.

Psychologists describe this as **identity foreclosure**: committing to an identity too early and living your life in service of protecting that image. For me, it was the "good" image, reliable, ethical, steady. But the danger of foreclosure is that it shuts down exploration. You don't ask who you *really* are; you only ask how to live up to the script.

Carl Jung called this the **persona**, the social mask carefully constructed to gain approval. But every mask has a cost. Behind it waits the **shadow**: the qualities, desires, impulses, and emotions that don't fit the "good" narrative. The anger, the selfishness, the playfulness, even the desire to rest. All the pieces are disowned in the name of "goodness."

Here lies what I call the *tyranny of the good self*: a life lived out of obedience, constantly policing oneself to avoid disapproval. It isn't true morality, but a *subtle imprisonment*. As **Brené Brown** reminds us, perfectionism isn't about excellence but about avoiding shame. For the "good one," every mistake feels like exposure, every slip a *threat to belonging.*

Sometimes, freedom first appears in the figure of the *outlaw*, the so-called *"villain."* In myth and psyche, the villain represents rebellion against imposed roles. When I see Raavan not just as "bad" but as *free*, I glimpse the possibility of *disidentification*: stepping away from the over-identified role of the "good one" and reclaiming personal choice.

In this light, the "bad" self isn't immoral; it's *bold, unapologetic, boundary-setting*. It doesn't corrupt; it liberates. **Jung** would call this **shadow integration**: welcoming back the parts of us we exiled, and discovering that they contain strength, not sin.

The practical truth is simple but hard: real freedom begins the moment you allow yourself to disappoint others in order to remain aligned with your own truth. And in that moment, being *"bad"* might be the most profoundly *goo*d thing you could ever do for yourself.

Symbolic Meaning

In mythology, **Raavan** isn't just a villain but an archetype of rebellion, a mirror of the repressed self. His unapologetic defiance symbolises the unlived freedom within us, the voice that dares to say, "I will not obey simply because obedience is expected."

The polarity of **good vs. bad** isn't a moral binary, but a psychological one. "Good" often means image-protecting obedience, living in line with expectations, keeping the mask intact. "Bad" means authentic freedom, stepping out of the mask, even if it risks being misunderstood.

When I look at my own life, I can see how symbolic events like the **collapse of my marriage** or the **loss of a job** were never just circumstantial; they were cracks in the "good son / good man" persona. They became initiations, forcing me to confront the shadow self I had kept buried.

Archetypally, this is a **death–rebirth moment**: the death of the false self (the obedient “good one”) and the birth of the authentic one (the integrated whole).

Sometimes, it is good to be bad, not because badness is the goal, but because freedom is.

The day you stop needing to be good in everyone’s story, you start becoming true in your own story.

And when the fire cools, its ashes settle in the body, waiting to be felt, remembered, and released.

Chapter Five

The Wisdom of the Body

"The body remembers what the mind forgets."

30. The Boy Who Refused to Be Cut Down

All through school, I was the *bright one.*

Class monitor for ten straight years.

Respected. Valued. Seen.

My *identity was woven* into those spaces of recognition and achievement.

When the 10th board exams approached, the principal called me in.

"We're counting on you to bring *laurels* to the school," he said.

It landed on my chest like a *medal.*

And I didn't disappoint.

I passed with strong marks, proud and ready for the next chapter—admission into class eleven.

My father came with me to the new school, carrying my documents, my marks, my effort, my story.

I had chosen both Maths and Biology, eager to explore the *logical* and the *living.*

We stepped into the principal's office.

He glanced at my form, looked up, and delivered his verdict:

"Students from your school are notorious. They don't do well in both Maths and Biology. He should drop one."

The words didn't just hurt, they *burned*.

How could he dismiss me without knowing me?

Wasn't my past performance proof enough?

How dare he underestimate me based on where I came from?

My father tried to reason.

"He may know better. He has experience," he said gently.

But I was adamant.

"No. I will keep both."

It wasn't just a choice.

It was *defiance*.

A *declaration*.

A desperate grasp to hold onto my worth.

For the next two years, I studied with a *quiet vengeance*.

Every late night, every page turned, was a silent retort to that moment in the principal's office.

And when the results came, I had my proof; I scored higher in Biology than in Math, even when Biology wasn't my cup of tea. I didn't enjoy it.

On paper, I had won.

But deep down, the wound remained.

The betrayal of being judged before being known.

The loneliness of stepping out of a small pond and being told I might not survive the ocean.

The ache of losing my *unquestioning belief* that effort alone could shield me from judgment.

Yes, I proved my capacity.

But I also learned that some *scars are written in ink no mark sheet can erase.*

Sacred Pause and Reflections

- Have you ever felt pressure to *shrink, hide, or soften yourself* to fit into others' *comfort zones?*
- When you *refused to shrink*, what did it cost you? And what did it *give* you?

Psychological Lens

When I look back at that boy who refused to be cut down, I see more than just stubbornness. I see the *raw human instinct to defend dignity.* Psychologists often note that defiance in childhood isn't always rebellion for its own sake; it can also be an early expression of *self-preservation,* a refusal to be diminished. In my case, standing tall in the face of being "cut down" wasn't about arrogance; it was about *survival of identity.*

Developmental psychology talks about **ego boundaries**, the invisible lines that define where "I" ends and the world begins. When those boundaries are threatened (through criticism, humiliation, or control), children often react with defiance, not because they want to oppose authority, but because they are trying to hold on to a sense of self. My refusal was my way of saying: *"I am here. I matter. You cannot erase me."*

At the same time, this defiance carried a cost. The energy that could have gone into curiosity, creativity, or play became invested in resistance. Psychologists call this **reactive identity formation**, shaping who you are mainly in response to what you are resisting. It gave me strength, yes, but it also tied my selfhood to opposition.

What I see now is that such defiance is a double-edged sword. It protects us when the world feels hostile, but it can also become a prison if we cling to it for too long. True freedom begins when the defiance softens, when we no longer need to fight to prove we exist, but can simply *inhabit our existence.*

Symbolic Meaning

Symbolically, the image of "refusing to be cut down" evokes the archetype of the **wounded rebel**, one who would rather endure pain than surrender autonomy. The *rope* becomes a metaphor for life's binding forces (rules, social roles, external control), and the boy's stance transforms it from an instrument of restraint into a statement of selfhood.

In mythic terms, this is the **trial of endurance**, a test where the hero proves worthiness not by defeating the external obstacle, but by holding onto the inner conviction that "my choice is mine to make."

The deeper takeaway: sometimes, in standing your ground, you are not resisting rescue; you are preserving the right to decide what *rescue* means.

31. The Question That Opened the Door

It began as a dream, not the fleeting kind that fades with morning light, but the kind that stays in your *bones*.

I wanted to create something bigger than myself.

Being a Reiki Master was fulfilling, but my soul wanted more: *more connection, more impact, more lives touched*. I imagined a space where healers from across the world could gather, share their gifts, and lift each other higher.

One quiet afternoon, the idea arrived like a whisper:

A Healing Conference.

A place for deep work, shared wisdom, and the kind of moments that change you without warning.

I named it *The Aha Moment*. I even designed the logo, a symbol of clarity and light.

When I told a close friend, her excitement was instant.

"We have to do this!" she said, and her enthusiasm breathed life into my idea.

Weeks later, she introduced me to a friend, a well-known therapist from Canada. She was warm, charismatic, and immediately on board. She even promised to bring in influential names to make the event extraordinary.

The three of us sat together, sketching plans, the website, the speakers, and the flow of the day. I felt my dream becoming real.

And then…

In the middle of the conversation, she turned to me with a simple question:

“So… what is Ankur going to do at the conference?”

It hit me like a punch to the chest.

For a moment, my brain scrambled for an answer, but all I could feel was the heat rising in my face. I opened my mouth, but nothing came out.

This was *my* idea. My creation. My vision.

Somewhere inside me, a quiet voice whispered:

She doesn't want to be the one who lit the match. She wanted me to stand in the fire.

Was I good enough to take that stage? Did I have anything worth giving? Or was I just someone who dreamed big but stayed small?

That night, I couldn't sleep.

I replayed the moment over and over, feeling both exposed and strangely grateful, because the discomfort was telling me something.

It was saying:

It isn't enough to create the space. You have to step into it.

From that day forward, I began collecting skills, Reiki, past life regression, family constellations, energy, and psychology. Not to impress. Not to prove. But to become someone who could stand before a room full of strangers and speak with the kind of authority that comes from *living your truth.*

One simple question had torn through my comfort zone.

And through that tear, my deeper path began to grow.

The conference never happened, never materialised.

But that moment created a place for me, a place that remains forever.

Sacred Pause and Reflections

- Has someone ever asked you a question that *pierced through your defences* and *revealed something about yourself?*
- When have you built something, an idea, a project, a dream, but hesitated to *step fully into it?*
- What is one *"door"* you're standing before right now, waiting for the courage to walk through?
- If someone asked you today, "What is your *role*?", how would you answer?

Psychological Lens

This story is a vivid example of the **Socratic method** in psychology, using open-ended, reflective questioning to invite self-discovery rather than prescribing answers. In therapy, this is aligned with **motivational interviewing** and **client-centred therapy** (**Carl Rogers**), where the role of the listener isn't to "fix" but to help the speaker access their own truth.

When someone asks a question that pierces through habitual narratives, it bypasses the **default mode network** (the brain's autopilot thinking) and forces the mind into a **metacognitive state**, thinking about one's own thinking. This is often the spark that leads to transformational insight.

From a trauma and identity perspective, such questions can also trigger **schema disruption** (**Jeffrey Young's Schema Therapy**). If someone's core schema is *"I am stuck"* or *"I am helpless,"* a well-placed question can destabilise that schema and allow for new possibilities to enter consciousness.

In the process of this learning, I realised something profound: the collection of expertise, certificates, and experiences was never about proving myself to anyone else. Instead, it was the universe's way of showing me how much there was still to learn, to live, and to integrate. It was a shift from *external validation to inner alignment.*

In hindsight, the *"conference"* was already happening *within me.* Each new skill, each lived experience, each stumble and rise was preparing me. The universe was *aligning me, building my inner ground,* before I could ever hold space for an outer conference.

Symbolic Meaning

Symbolically, the *"door"* in the title represents the **threshold between unconscious patterns and conscious choice**. The question functions as a **key**, small in form, but powerful enough to open something vast. In myth and archetype, the "wise question" is a common motif; think of the Sphinx's riddle in Greek mythology or the koans in Zen Buddhism.

In this frame, the person asking the question plays the role of the **threshold guardian**, not blocking the way, but ensuring the traveller is ready to step through with awareness. The transformation doesn't come from the answer itself, but from the act of pausing to seek it within.

The essence of the story is this: in the right moment, a single sincere question can act as a **psychological initiator**, inviting us into a new chapter of our inner journey.

32. When Devotion Turns into Arrogance

It began in *sincerity.*

An astrologer, trusted by many, had advised me to take up a 108-day ritual.

A spiritual *sadhana* to shift my personal circumstances.

And so, I did.

With full heart.

With unwavering discipline.

With a devotion sharp as a blade and *precise as breath.*

Day after day, I showed up.

Some days were soft. Some were restless. Some were soaked in longing.

But I kept going.

Ninety days passed. Ninety-five. Ninety-eight. Almost a hundred.

And then… the question rose.

What has changed?

No miracle.

No breakthrough.

No jackpot from heaven.

Life, it seemed, continued its ordinary, *unspectacular rhythm.*

I was still doing the ritual, but the spark of early surrender had faded.
Something in me had shifted, quietly, almost invisibly.

The chant had become a *checklist.*

The offering, a *silent demand.*

One morning, I finally asked, really asked:

"Why am I doing this? What am I expecting from you?"

And in the stillness that followed, an answer came, not in thunder, not in visions, but in a whisper that wrapped itself around my heart:

"The way you're doing this… isn't surrender. It's arrogance."

"You've begun to say: I am doing this. I am devoted. I am disciplined. And now, You, God, must *change my life."*

When did my devotion turn into a *transaction?*

When did my faith carry the hidden clause: *Because I worked hard, you must deliver*?

I saw it clearly, painfully:

I wasn't praying anymore.

I was bargaining.

Not worshipping: *I was negotiating.*

What I called "faith" had calcified into spiritual pride:

"Look how devoted I am"

"Look how consistent I've been."

"Surely you must notice."

I had mistaken *discipline* for *devotion.*

Persistence for *purity.*

And so I whispered:

"God… I need a master.

Someone who can pull me out of this trap.

Someone who can crack open this *spiritual ego* and show me the *naked truth* again."

But before the prayer could fade, another voice came, gentle, amused, almost playful:

"If you were rejecting MY presence… then who just answered you?"

That question undid me.

Tears came, uninvited, unstoppable.

The very *presence* I thought I had lost… had been here *all along.*

The dialogue I thought I was starting… was perhaps being guided from the other side from the *very first day*.

The prayer had never stopped working.

It wasn't changing my circumstances.

It was *changing me.*

Sacred Pause and Reflections

- When has your *spiritual* practice brought you closer to *humility*, and when has it fed your *pride*?
- Do you sometimes seek recognition for your *faith*, *kindness*, or *service*, rather than *simply offering it?*

Psychological Lens

This story beautifully exposes a phenomenon in spiritual practice known as **spiritual materialism**, a term popularised by **Chögyam Trungpa**. It describes when the *ego* co-opts spiritual discipline for its own agenda, turning surrender into a subtle form of *control.*

I began with pure *intrinsic motivation*; the ritual was done out of devotion. But as days passed without visible results, the practice shifted into *extrinsic expectation: "I am doing this, so life must change.*" This is akin to the *effort–reward imbalance* model from occupational psychology, when one expects proportional returns for effort, frustration sets in if the outcome is delayed. In spirituality, that mindset becomes a transactional contract with the divine.

What's fascinating is the moment of realisation: "*The way you're doing this... isn't surrender.* It's *arrogance.*" This reflects a high level of *metacognition*, the ability to observe one's own thought patterns and catch the *ego's infiltration*. Psychologically, this is a **disidentification process from the ego state**, moving from *"I am my devotion"* to *"I am the observer of how devotion is being used."*

The dialogue with God, "If I were rejecting God's presence, then who just answered me?", touches on *Self–Self dialogue* in Jungian terms. The *"God"* voice here could be seen as the *deeper Self*, the inner source of wisdom, breaking through the *ego's script*.

Psychologically, we can explain it in many ways, but what matters is Faith. My mother used to tell a story. A devoted man spent many days worshipping his Lord Krishna statue, praying tirelessly for a sign. Yet, the deity never appeared. Eventually, frustrated by the silence, the man threw the stone idol out the window.

A little later, he lit a stick of incense inside. As the fragrant smoke rose, he glanced out the window and noticed the smoke drifting directly into the statue's nostrils.

A sudden, fierce conviction hit him. "Aha! So you *do* like the smell!" he muttered.

Driven by this simple thought, he rushed outside, took a small piece of cotton, and gently placed it in the statue's nostrils, as if protecting a living person from the smoke. At that very moment, Lord Krishna appeared before him.

The astonished man fell to his knees. "Why today, Lord? I threw you out! Why didn't you appear when I worshipped you for months?"

The Lord smiled. "I appeared today because today you truly saw me. All those months, you treated me like a statue you hoped would become real. But when you put the cotton in my nostrils, you finally *acknowledged that I was alive.* You realised I existed, and that simple realisation—that act of real faith—is all it ever took."

Symbolic Meaning

The 108-day ritual is a **sacred container**, symbolically representing the *mandala* of discipline, devotion, and *cyclical transformation.* In Hindu and Buddhist cosmology, 108 is a cosmic number, the completion of a spiritual cycle.

The shift from surrender to arrogance mirrors the **myth of *Icarus***, starting with the blessing of wings (devotion), but flying too close to the sun (*ego expectation*) and risking a fall. Here, the "fall" isn't dramatic failure, but the *soft disillusionment* when God doesn't play by the *ego's* rules.

The whisper from God is the **trickster element** in mythology, the divine refusing to meet the human on transactional terms, instead revealing that presence was never absent. This is also the archetypal **return of the Beloved**, not as an external miracle, but as the realisation that the relationship itself is the miracle.

The tears at the end signal the **collapse of the spiritual persona**, the mask of "I am the devoted one", and the emergence of genuine *humility*. In **psychological transformation** models, this is the moment where the ***ego*** shifts from controlling the divine to being guided by the *deeper Self.*

33. The Girl at the Coffee Shop

One afternoon, I opened my LinkedIn inbox to find an unusual message from a girl who wanted to meet me.

She explained she had come across my profile,

but not on LinkedIn.

On a *matrimonial* website.

The only problem?

The profile was a mess, full of false details, cobbled together without my knowledge by my brother-in-law. (It wrongly listed me as an admin manager.) Yet, somehow, she'd cut through the noise, found the real me, and reached out directly.

I admired that.

It takes *courage to walk toward clarity* when confusion would have been the easier option.

We agreed to meet at a coffee shop in Gurgaon.

I was already seated on the raised section when she walked in, funny, lively, quick with her words. The kind of person who could make strangers feel like old friends within minutes.

But underneath that sparkle, I noticed something else.

A weight in her eyes.

A kind of *sadness so well-hidden that only someone who's carried their own could recognise it.*

Her humour wasn't just charm, it was armour.

We didn't waste time with pleasantries.

"Are you seriously looking to get married?" she asked,

"Or just exploring options?"

"Exploring," I said honestly.

Then I turned the question back to her:

"Why do *you* want to get married?"

She looked at me as if I'd just asked why the sun rises.

"What kind of question is that? Everyone gets married!"

"Not the societal answer," I said. "Think for yourself. Why do *you* want to get married?"

She didn't answer that day.

A few days later, she reached out again. Her voice was different, quieter, more *vulnerable*.

She told me she had been married before.

Her husband had died of cancer while still young. She had cared for him until his last breath. After his death, her family, fearful of losing her too, became overprotective, almost suffocating.

For her, marriage wasn't about romance at all.

It was an *escape*.

A doorway to freedom, she didn't feel she could walk through on her own.

We didn't marry.

We both knew we wanted different things in a partner.

But something unexpected grew in that space,

not a romance, but a *therapeutic relationship*.

I walked beside her for a while, not as a suitor, but as a *friend, a guide, a mirror.* I helped her find a deeper reason to love again, one rooted in desire, not in escape.

And one day, she married again.

Not to run from something,

but to *walk toward it.*

Sacred Pause and Reflections

- Before making *major life* decisions (getting married, a job, choosing a major to study, or having a baby), have I ever paused to ask myself, *"Why do I want this?"*
- What role does *courage* play in walking toward *clarity* when *confusion seems easier?*

Psychological Lens

This story opens a window into **attachment theory (Bowlby, 1969**) and how loss, grief, and control intersect in human relationships. The girl's initial desire for marriage wasn't rooted in romantic longing but in the search for **emotional liberation** from an overprotective family system. In psychological terms, her motive was more about **escape-avoidance coping** than **approach-motivation** (seeking love for its own sake).

Her humour and vibrancy in the meeting may have functioned as a **defence mechanism**, specifically **reaction formation**, where a person displays exaggerated positivity to mask underlying vulnerability or sadness. It's a socially acceptable way of protecting oneself from deeper emotional exposure during first encounters.

For me, the meeting becomes a kind of therapeutic intervention. This shifts the dynamic from a transactional search for a partner to a transformational connection that addresses core needs. In **Gestalt terms**, I acted as a *catalyst for awareness*, helping her move from *"marriage as escape"* to *"marriage as conscious choice."*

Symbolic Meaning

The coffee shop serves as a **neutral ground**, neither her controlled family home nor his personal space. Symbolically, coffee shops in stories often represent **transitional spaces** where transformation begins, much like train stations or waiting rooms. Here, it becomes the stage where the "false profile" is replaced by a real human exchange.

The act of tracking him down on LinkedIn despite the wrong matrimonial profile speaks to the archetype of **the seeker**, someone willing to navigate obstacles to reach what they want. However, the initial "quest" was toward a goal (marriage) that didn't fully match her inner readiness. The story arc shifts when she receives guidance to look inward first.

Her journey echoes the mythological motif of **the threshold guardian**, the person (in this case, the narrator) who appears before a major life transition, not to offer the desired reward, but to ensure the seeker is truly ready for it.

34. The Day I Never Bunked Again

I don' t remember my exact age, between 9 to 11 years old, but I remember the feeling, a stubborn, tearful certainty that today, of all days, I couldn't go to school. My tears flowed with a kind of dramatic power, a tantrum meant to *water the whole street*, and in my small, tear-soaked world, I was sure the earth would halt its rotation just for me.

It didn't.

The school bus pulled up, and my mother, a woman who had seen me through countless battles, marched me to its front door. She pushed me inside, and in that moment, I heard the muffled giggles from the bus.

The other kids, perched high in their seats, watched my drama unfold. Their *laughter stung* more than any scolding. My mother, with a swiftness

I still cannot explain, came down from the other side, her face a stern mask as she sealed the "trick" of getting me on the bus.

But I had a trick of my own. I stayed hidden, curled in my seat, a small act of rebellion, and let the bus carry me right back home.

My mother was washing clothes, the *rhythmic slap* of fabric on stone the only sound. Our eyes met across the courtyard. She knew. I knew. And in that moment of silent communication, I knew I was doomed.

Her eyes held a *deep fear*, not just of my defiance, but of a future she desperately wanted to prevent. She had seen too many people in our village end up picking up *cow dung,* their lives swallowed by the *smallness of their circumstances*. She was terrified I would become one of them, that my small act of rebellion was a seed of a much larger failure. *To her, my rebellion* wasn't *about a single day; it was the seed of a wasted life.*

That day, three sticks broke across my legs. She locked me in the old storeroom, the one that smelled of *dust, onions, and forgotten summers,* and told me to follow my school timetable, period by period. "You'll get food at recess," she said, her voice like a judge announcing a final sentence. I cried until the air felt heavy and suffocating.

And then, my grandfather appeared, my *unexpected rescuer*. He scolded my mother for her harshness, took my small hand, and began the long walk to school.

Four kilometres, uphill. When we reached, my class was outside being punished, the girls with their hands raised, the boys in the dreaded *murga* position.

My grandfather explained to the teacher that I couldn't make it on time, so he had brought me himself. The teacher nodded, and sent my grandfather home… and promptly told me to join the punishment line.

Punished at home. Punished at school. The great double feature of childhood justice.

And yet, later that day, I scored 25 out of 25 in a math test.

I skipped home, yes, skipped, clutching my paper like a victory flag.

I showed my mother, expecting her to melt. She did smile. She did soften.

She told me why showing up to school mattered, her fear replaced with a glimmer of pride.

I never bunked again, not in school, not in college, not at work.

Even now, I rarely take leave. *That day branded me with a lifelong lesson: showing up is non-negotiable.*

Sacred Pause and Reflections

- When in your life did *punishment, shame,* or *struggle* paradoxically become the *seed* of a *strength*?
- Do you carry habits *born more from fear or from pride?*
- If you traced your *strongest discipline* back to its *roots*, would you find *love*, *fear*, or some *potent mix of both?*

Psychological Lens

At first glance, this is a story about skipping school and getting punished. But beneath it, it's really a story of how *discipline, fear, pride,* and *generational trauma intertwined* to shape a lifelong habit.

Psychologically, two major forms of conditioning were at play. Through **operant conditioning (B.F. Skinner)**, every act of bunking was paired with immediate negative consequences: a stick across the legs at home, public humiliation in the "murga" position, and the sting of being laughed at by peers. These punishments worked as powerful negative reinforcers, teaching me that skipping obligations would always invite pain and shame.

At the same time, **classical conditioning (Ivan Pavlov)** was quietly at work. School itself became associated not only with punishment avoidance but also with moments of pride, like scoring full marks on that math test. Over time, the brain began to encode "showing up" as not only the safer option, but also the one linked to competence and worth. The result was a deeply ingrained behavioural loop: *always show up, never skip.*

From the lens of **schema therapy (Jeffrey Young)**, this moment planted the seeds of a *"Responsibility schema",* the belief that safety, worth, and even love come only from fulfilling duties with consistency. Such a schema can become a strength, manifesting as reliability and discipline. Yet it can also harden, leaving little room for rest, play, or rebellion without guilt. The freedom to pause becomes overshadowed by the compulsion to keep proving oneself responsible.

But behind my punishment was another story, not just mine, but my mother's. Her fear of a *"small life"* for me was the *hidden fuel.* She had seen what poverty, limitation, and missed opportunities could do. In her hands, the stick wasn't only a tool of control but an expression of *fear-driven love.* She beat me not only to correct me but to ward off the destiny she dreaded for me. In this sense, her actions carried the weight of *generational trauma,* the transmission of unhealed fears and limitations from one life into another.

And so, the lesson etched into me that day wasn't just about bunking school. It was about survival, aspiration, and the *invisible hand* of ancestral fear shaping discipline. The bruises faded, but the deeper imprint, the vow to *always show up,* stayed. The question that remains is whether this vow is my own… or whether it's *my mother's fear, still living through me.*

Symbolical Meaning

The events of that day can be read as more than punishment or discipline; they form a *mythic arc,* mirroring the **Hero's Journey archetype:**

The *Call to Responsibility* – The simple summons to attend school is the call to step into duty and growth.

The *Refusal of the Call* – Hiding in the bus is the avoidance, the first instinct to escape the path of challenge.

The *Road of Trials* – The double punishment, at home and at school, becomes the initiation. Two guardians stand at the threshold, testing my resilience: family and society, both demanding accountability.

The *Threshold Guide* – My grandfather plays the role of the quiet mentor. He points me back toward the path but doesn't shield me from the trials awaiting. His guidance is gentle, but it preserves the integrity of the journey.

The *Boon or Treasure* – The perfect score on the math test emerges as the reward, the unexpected treasure wrestled from the hardship. It transforms the day of humiliation into a story of pride and redemption.

Seen this way, my mother isn't only a disciplinarian but also the **threshold guardian**, embodying the paradox of fear and love. My grandfather is the mentor who supports but doesn't rescue. And the math test is the boon, proof that suffering and perseverance can yield pride and strength.

The day I bunked became the day I never bunked again. It was less about obedience and more about initiation, a personal *rite of passage* teaching me the truth: *life rewards those who show up*.

35. The Woman Who Made Time Wait

We were supposed to be heading to a project meeting, the kind that carries the smell of new beginnings, the *quiet thrill of possibility.*

I stood by the lift, pressing the button. Once. Twice. A third time.

Twelve minutes passed.

No sign of her.

Finally, I sent a message:

"I am going to the basement to get the car. Meet me at the reception."

This wasn't the first time.

I thought of all those evenings parked outside her mother's house, engine running, headlights soft against the wall. Me, *ready. Waiting.*

And her?

She would step out, smile, then slip back inside, water to drink, fruit to pack, something she had "just forgotten." Always *one more thing.*

It had seemed harmless then. A quirk. But over the years, I began to notice a thread running through these moments: I was always the one waiting.

And today, it happened again, though in a stranger way.

She made lunch for herself and our son. Set it on the table. Then… left it there, walking outside to hang the laundry.

Even the *food was made to wait.*

Was this simply a habit?

Or… was there something unspoken underneath?

Maybe, somewhere deep down, making time wait for her was a way of *reclaiming worth.* A subtle proof to herself that *she mattered,* that her arrival could pause the clock, tilt the rhythm of someone else's day. A small, almost invisible rebellion in a world that often rushes women past their *own presence.*

Or maybe it had nothing to do with power.

Maybe it was her nervous system, delaying arrival because full presence feels *too sudden, too exposing.*

And then, as always, the *mirror turned back toward me.*

Why does this stir me so deeply? Why do I take it so personally?

Because I have spent my life trying to be the "on-time" one. The prepared one. The one who shows respect by being ready.

And when I am kept waiting, it feels as if my effort, my quiet discipline, has gone *unseen*.

But perhaps the real question isn't about her pace or mine.

Perhaps it's this:

What if I let go of being "the one who waits" *or* "the one who is waited for"?

What if I simply *arrived*, wherever I am, *fully*?

Sacred Pause and Reflections

- When someone keeps you waiting, what emotions rise in you: *impatience*, *hurt, anger,* or the *quiet ache of feeling unimportant?*
- For you, is arriving on time *simply a habit, a sign of respect,* or *also a shield* that hides a deeper wound, perhaps the fear of being dismissed or overlooked?
- Do you *secretly measure your worth* by how others *honour your time?* And if so, what happens when that "measure" isn't met?

Psychological Lens

To move deeper, we can ask: Is this really about time or about what time represents in a relationship?

At its core, this story isn't really about minutes lost or clocks ignored; It's about identity, value, and the subtle pervasive *temporal power dynamic* in relationships. Chronic lateness or delay, especially in intimate contexts, can be a form of *micro-behavioural assertion,* a low-intensity way of reclaiming agency when one feels overpowered or undervalued elsewhere. Psychologists sometimes frame this under *passive-aggressive behaviour* or *nonconscious boundary-setting.*

From an **attachment theory** perspective, these repeated delays could reflect an *avoidant coping style.* Arriving late may delay intimacy or emotional exposure, acting as a small shield against being fully "present" in moments that might feel demanding. For some, it's also a subtle way of controlling the rhythm of interaction, ensuring that the other person is waiting, which symbolically confirms their importance.

By arriving late, one partner delays **emotional exposure and intimacy**, using time as a shield. It also reshapes the rhythm of interaction: one person waits, the other arrives. Waiting becomes a *symbolic confirmation of importance*, a subtle way of reinforcing one's presence and power.

On the other side of this dynamic, my experience is deeply psychological. I cannot help but watch the clock; I cannot help but feel the *rising agitation.* For me, punctuality isn't just a habit; It's *identity.* I have built my self-concept around being dependable, respectful, present. So, when I am left waiting, it doesn't just test my patience; it creates a *psychological split* inside me. On one side is my self-image: dependable, respectful, present. On the other hand, is the lived experience of being *disregarded* in that very moment. Psychologists call this *cognitive dissonance,* the inner discomfort when identity and reality collide. In my case, it sharpens into an **identity–value conflict**: I value respect, I practice it through punctuality, but when that value isn't reciprocated, I feel *unacknowledged.* What might look like a minor delay on the surface is, inside, a quiet questioning of my *worth and visibility.*

Importantly, both behaviours can be *self-reinforcing.* Her lateness may unconsciously affirm her sense of worth, and my punctuality affirms my sense of integrity. Without awareness, they lock into a complementary pattern that repeats. The conflict isn't about time at all. It's about what time *symbolises in the silent dialogue between two psyches.*

Symbolic Meaning

Symbolically, *time* here is the real currency, not minutes or hours, but **presence and significance**. In Jungian terms, “making time wait” can be seen as a ritual of *self-affirmation*, where the individual bends the collective order (time) to their own pace, thus reclaiming sovereignty.

The laundry left hanging while the food waits is especially telling; It's as though even nourishment, a primal symbol of care, must pause until *her* sequence is complete. This transforms an everyday act into a symbolic declaration: “I will set the order of things.”

For me, waiting becomes more than physical idleness; It's a **liminal state** where my own self-worth is silently tested. In myth, waiting at thresholds is often the hero's trial, a pause before action that reveals inner patterns more than outer events.

If both partners can see this pattern, the act of "waiting" could shift from a silent power struggle to a **shared ritual of presence**, where arrival isn't about dominance but about meeting fully, without the residue of control or resentment.

And in listening to the body, we hear whispers of time and death, reminders that every ending carries a gift.

Chapter Six

The Gift of a Symbolic Death

"To die before we die is to discover how to live."

36. The Gift of Death

Death has always fascinated me, not in a morbid way, but as a *doorway.*

A mystery that asks more questions than it answers.

That fascination deepened when I began my work as a past life regression therapist and stepped into my own past lives.

The very first life I saw was as a king.

I sat on a heap of dead bodies, sword in hand, my heart *heavy with guilt.*

The battlefield was silent, but my mind roared with regret.

I had won the war, but at what cost?

That image etched itself into me.

And suddenly, parts of my current life made sense: how easily I sink into guilt, how naturally I carry the *burden of self-blame.*

It wasn't new. It was ancient.

In another life, I longed to become a monk.

But my mother's fierce, protective love held me back.

That yearning for the spiritual path went unfulfilled.

Strangely enough, in this life, that same soul returned as my current wife, which I learned during my 10-day Vipassana meditation in India.

She brought me to Vietnam, the land of Buddhism, unknowingly helping me fulfil that *karmic longing.*

The soul always finds its way.

Through all these soul journeys, I've never feared death itself.

What I feared was the process of dying, the pain, the *helplessness*, the possibility of becoming a *burden* in this life.

But when I looked closer, I saw the truth:

It wasn't the pain I feared.

It was the thought of being in pain *without money.*

The fear of being *dependent*, financially and physically, ran deeper than pride.

It was an *old wound.*

The same wound that taught me, lifetime after lifetime, that my soul's real work isn't in avoiding death… but in learning how to meet death *without the weight of pain.*

Sacred Pause and Reflections

- When you think about death, what is it that you *actually fear, the moment of dying,* or *what comes before it?*
- Have you ever carried *guilt from choices you made (or didn't make)* long ago? How has that guilt shaped *your present life?*
- What is the one thing you want to do *before you die?*

Psychological Lens

This story isn't only about death but about the *echoes of death* across lifetimes. What surfaced in the regression wasn't fear of dying; it was the *unfinished emotional residue*: guilt from past violence, longing from denied paths, and the *shame of dependency*. Psychologists today might describe these as **core emotional imprints**, beliefs and feelings so deeply embedded that they outlive circumstances, often replaying in different forms across time.

The battlefield vision reveals **transgenerational guilt** in psychological terms, a burden that feels larger than one lifetime. Carrying the weight of blame becomes second nature, almost like a default lens through which present experiences are filtered. In psychodynamic language, this is *introjection*, taking responsibility for suffering, even when it doesn't wholly belong to us.

The second memory, of yearning for a monk's path but being stopped by love, brings up the tension between **autonomy and attachment**, a universal conflict. What fascinates me is how it looped back: the same soul, now in this life as a wife, guided me to Vietnam, to the very spiritual ground that once felt out of reach. This reflects Jung's idea of the **psyche as self-regulating**, that what is left unfinished seeks completion, often in surprising ways.

But the most piercing realisation came not from the soul journeys, but from the present fear: not the fear of death, but the fear of dying *without money*. Here, money becomes more than currency; it becomes the symbol of dignity, independence, and respect. Psychologists sometimes frame this through the lens of **shame as a self-conscious emotion** (**Lewis, 1971**), a painful awareness of self when we imagine how others might see us. In this context, needing money is equated with being *"less than"*, a psychological shorthand meaning diminished in *dignity, status, or worth*. It carries the feeling that dependence doesn't just limit one's freedom, but also makes one appear smaller, weaker, almost reduced in value in the eyes of others. That is why the fear of pain was tolerable, but the fear of dependence was unbearable.

Seen this way, death itself was never the enemy. The deeper wound was *shame*, the silent belief that love and respect are lost when one becomes dependent. And the healing isn't about avoiding death, but about releasing *shame* so that when the final moment arrives, it can be met without the weight of *unworthiness*.

Symbolic Meaning

The *"king"* can be seen as the *ego in a position of control*, while *"death"* is the archetypal **Wise Elder**, the one truth the ego cannot escape. In many mythic traditions, kings are often humbled by encounters with death, learning that their power is temporary and their real legacy lies not in control but in *conscious, compassionate choice.*

37. The Lover of Pain

In my youth, I never understood why pain felt like a *familiar friend.*

Not the kind that bruises the skin, the kind that leaves *fingerprints on the heart.*

While others chased love, I chased the ache that came after it.

Maybe it was because I loved writing poems, not just any poems, but sad ones.

The kind where longing curls into every line, where heartbreak hums between the words.

There are only so many words in the world…

And yet poets could take the same ones and spin them into something that slices the soul open.

Everyone has their own style.

Mine was pain.

But here's the thing, poems like that don't come from thin air.

I had to *feel* them.

So, I would close my eyes and *summon pain like an old companion.*

I'd imagine myself in a dark room, knees to my chest, tears streaming down my face.

I'd whisper the question that seemed to unlock the floodgates:

Why me?

And then… the words would come.

I thought I was just writing.

I didn't realise I was also… scripting.

Years later, life began handing me scenes I had already written.

One by one, the sad poems stepped off the page and into my reality.

My divorce.

Heartbreaks.

Moments where my world collapsed in silence.

Even before I entered my marriage, I knew, deep down, it *wouldn't last.*

But intuition speaks in whispers, and I was skilled at ignoring whispers.

I remember one poem in particular.

I had described myself exactly as life later placed me:

In a dark room.

Curled up.

Sobbing.

Thinking, *why me?*

It was eerie, as if life had been reading from my notebook.

That's when I understood:

Sometimes, we don't just write poetry.

Sometimes, *poetry writes us*.

Sacred Pause and Reflections

- The story suggests we can be *addicted to our own suffering.* How have you seen this *pattern* show up in your life or in the lives of those you know?
- Do you *secretly fear* who you might be *without your pain,* or what life would *demand of you if you were free from it?*

Psychological Lens

At first, this story might seem like it's about poetry. But beneath the words, it reveals a deeper pattern: how pain can become not just an experience but an *identity*. In psychology, this is often linked to what's called **negative affectivity**, a tendency to dwell on sadness, longing, or hurt, and in doing so, unconsciously reinforce them.

When I say I loved pain more than love itself, I was describing what therapists sometimes recognise as **emotional conditioning**. Because I only wrote poetry when I visualised myself in pain, my brain wired creativity and suffering together. Neuroscience calls this **Hebbian learning**: neurons that fire together, wire together. Over time, the act of writing poetry became inseparable from imagining heartbreak. What began as an artistic ritual grew into a psychological rehearsal. I wasn't just *expressing* pain through poems; I was *training* myself to inhabit it.

This also echoes the **Zeigarnik effect**: the mind's tendency to keep unfinished emotional "loops" alive. Each unwritten stanza, each incomplete vision of sorrow, left a residue. My unconscious then sought situations in real life to finish those poems. Divorce, heartbreak, loneliness, they were not random; they were *enactments of the imagery* I had once rehearsed. In this way, imagination became prophecy.

There's also a deeper attachment thread. Psychologists studying **self-identity and suffering** note that sometimes people cling to pain because it provides coherence. Joy can feel fleeting, unstable, even undeserved, but pain feels *solid, dependable, familiar*. In my case, pain became a companion, a muse, almost a lover. It was the shadow that promised permanence when everything else was uncertain.

Modern therapies like **Internal Family Systems (IFS)** would call this a **"part",** a part of me that clung to suffering because it believed suffering kept me safe, creative, and connected to meaning. That part didn't want me to heal, because healing threatened its role. But IFS also teaches that every part, even the lover of pain, has a positive intention. Pain was trying to give me depth, beauty, and a sense of control over chaos; it just didn't know any other way.

Ultimately, the Lover of Pain is a mirror of **self-avoidance**: it kept me busy with sorrow so I didn't have to face the *terror of emptiness*. But healing begins when pain is no longer the only doorway to creativity or depth. When I can write from joy, from wonder, from gratitude, then I am no longer enslaved by the shadow.

Symbolic Meaning

Pain in this context acts like a **familiar lover**; it wounds and comforts at the same time. Symbolically, It's the hearth we return to, even when the fire burns us, because we fear the *coldness of the unknown*. True healing requires *the courage to "break up" with that lover* and learn *intimacy with peace*, something that initially feels foreign but eventually becomes the new home.

38. The Midnight Call

It was a normal evening.

Dinner. A movie. The *quiet slide toward sleep.*

Then my phone rang. When the phone rings at midnight, the *body knows before the mind*; it's never good news.

I hesitated, then answered.

"Ankur sir…"

The voice trembled.

It was one of my team members, a quiet man I'd barely spoken to, the kind who kept to himself in every meeting.

My first thought: something urgent at work.

But then he said, haltingly, "No… it isn't about work. I… I wanted to commit suicide. I didn't know who else to call. I only thought about you."

Pin drop silence.

We'd barely spoken before.

Why me?

What had I done to earn this *fragile trust* in his most desperate hour?

I didn't ask.

Instead, I stayed with him.

Listening.

Letting him *empty the weight* he had been carrying.

For over an hour, the darkness between us was filled with words, silences, and the *faint thread of human connection*.

By the end, he said he felt lighter.

He could sleep now.

I, on the other hand, *couldn't.*

Long after I hung up, his voice stayed with me, the tremor, the confession, the trust.

his girlfriend left him without closure...

People carry *storms you will never see* unless you are the one they choose to call when the night is at its darkest.

Sacred Pause and Reflections

- What is a story from your life where a *late-night phone call or text message changed everything?*
- How do you respond when life asks you to hold *responsibility* you *don't feel fully ready for?*

Psychological Lens

That phone ringing at midnight did more than disturb my sleep; it disturbed my *sense of safety.* In psychology, this kind of heightened alertness is often linked to **anticipatory anxiety**, the fear of what *might* happen before anything actually does. My body was already rehearsing disaster before I even picked up the call.

What I was experiencing is close to what clinicians call **hypervigilance**, an exaggerated state of sensory sensitivity, where the nervous system is constantly *scanning for threat*. It's common in people who have lived with unpredictability or sudden shocks in their past. The brain, shaped by those experiences, begins to equate silence with "calm before the storm" and night with danger. A ringing phone at midnight doesn't just signal communication; it signals crisis.

From a relational perspective, such reactions also reveal the **internalised scripts** we carry about responsibility. For me, a part of my mind whispered: *"If the phone is ringing, something must be wrong, and I must fix it."* This isn't just anxiety; It's also **role conditioning**, the invisible contract of being the one who responds, who manages, who holds others when chaos arrives.

And yet, that night became more than anxiety. The call, and my response, made me feel that I had saved a life. For the first time, I touched the sense that perhaps even serving *one life is enough to give my existence meaning*. A strange peace entered: *if I die tomorrow, at least I have done this.*

Years later, in an interview for an agile coaching role, a coach asked me: *"When did you first feel you became a coach?"* I didn't answer him directly.

But inside, I knew, it was that night. Not in a training room, not with certificates, but in the rawness of midnight, with fear on one side and service on the other. That was the moment

I realised I had stepped onto the path of being a coach, not because I had knowledge, but because I had chosen to *show up for another human life.*

39. The One Who Sees, But Waits

Since I was young, I've had ideas, wild, sharp, almost *prophetic ideas*.

They would spark from nowhere, catching the scent of something in the air that others had not yet noticed.

I could *feel* them, trends that were coming, movements that were inevitable.

And time after time, I watched those ideas appear in the market…

Three years later.

Five years later.

Not by me, but by someone who moved faster, *stayed longer, finished.*

It stings.

There was the training and development company I once dreamed of.

I even started it. It collapsed before it could breathe.

Then the gaming startup, something I *knew* would explode.

It did.

But without me. My friends rode that *wave* while I stood on the *shore*.

And now… I am here, writing my third book.

A book braided from my inner journey, my lived truths.

But that familiar voice returns:

Will this, too, be another unfinished chapter?

Another idea left to ripen in someone else's hands?

I don't know if this is self-sabotage, poor timing, or the quiet comfort of preparation that never becomes execution.

Maybe it's fear, of success, of failure, of the *grief that comes when the thing you imagined finally meets reality* and looks different from the dream.

Or maybe… I simply love *potential* more than I love *process*.

But this pattern itches.

It stalks me.

And maybe that's the sign, it's time to break it.

To act, not perfectly, not when I am "ready," but *now*.

To finish what I started.

To let the work be *messy and alive* instead of *immaculate in my head*.

Because in the end, what hurts most isn't failure.

It's the *echo of things I knew before the world did,*

and never claimed it as mine.

Sacred Pause and Reflections

- Have you ever seen an idea you once dreamed of nurtured and brought to life by someone else, and felt the ache of wishing you had claimed it as yours? What did that moment teach you about *hesitation, courage, or timing*?
- Can you remember a moment when you clearly saw what needed to be done, yet *held yourself back from acting*?
- Do you sometimes tell yourself you are *"waiting for the right time,"* when in truth you are *avoiding the risk of acting?*

Psychological Lens

This story reflects what psychologists call **analysis paralysis**, a recurring loop where vision and ideation run far ahead of action. Again and again, I find myself being the one who sees early but acts late. Outwardly, it looks like procrastination, but beneath the surface, it carries the weight of perfectionism and fear.

Procrastination is often dismissed as laziness, but research, like Piers Steel's *Procrastination Equation*, shows it's usually a **fear-based coping strategy**. Sometimes it's fear of failure: *If I try and fail, I lose the safety of being someone who "could have" done it.* Other times, it's fear of success: *If I succeed, expectations will rise to a level I may not be able to sustain.* Either way, the act of waiting protects me from being exposed.

I also recognise **self-handicapping** here. By delaying, by not putting my full effort in, I create a buffer: if failure comes, I can blame the lack of effort instead of questioning my ability. This preserves my self-esteem in the short term, but the price is heavy: unfulfilled visions and projects left undone.

At a deeper level, there's the **narrative I keep rehearsing** about myself: *I am the one who sees, but* doesn't *claim.* From a **narrative therapy perspective**, this storyline itself becomes dangerous. By telling and retelling it, I risk creating a self-fulfilling prophecy. My identity splits: one part visionary, one part avoider. And oddly enough, it's the completion, the finishing, that feels threatening. Because finishing dismantles the identity I have come to know: the observer, the one with potential, not the one with proof.

In truth, the waiting isn't just about time. It's about *identity*. To act is to risk reshaping who I am, moving from dreamer to doer. And sometimes, the familiar comfort of *waiting* feels safer than the unknown responsibility of *becoming*.

Symbolic Meaning

Symbolically, this is the archetype of **The Seer**, a figure present in many mythologies who perceives truths and future possibilities, yet struggles to act on them or embody them. In Greek myth, **Cassandra** foresaw the future yet couldn't act on it meaningfully. My curse has been quieter but similar: I trusted the *visions*, but not myself as their *vessel* to bring them to life.

The "half-lived dreams" in my story are like *ghosts in the psyche*, unfinished presences that linger, draining energy until they are either completed or consciously released. Each one is an unfinished bridge, suspended in midair, connecting me to a future I never crossed into.

The itch I feel now is the archetypal **call to individuation** (Jung), to stop hovering at the edge of potential and instead step into embodiment. It's also the beginning of **self-authorship**: rewriting the inner script from "the one who waits" into "the one who builds."

And the antidote is simple: *small, imperfect action*. In mythic language, the hero must take a step onto the bridge without knowing if the other side exists, trusting that the act of walking will help it appear.

40. The Echo of a Casual Wish

In my youth, when life felt like an open road and every evening was dipped in laughter, intensity, and *spiritual curiosity*, I would sometimes toss out a line:

"I don't want to live long, maybe till 45, and that's enough."

I cannot say if I truly meant it. Maybe it was just *philosophical bravado*, a way to sound detached.

Maybe… I did mean it a little.

But I've come to believe the *universe listens*, especially to the things we say with emotional charge, even if we disguise them as jokes.

Years passed.

Jobs came and went.

I touched spiritual highs and wrestled with *emotional shadows*.

At 44, nearly 45, I flew to Miri, Malaysia, to look after my brother-in-law's son while he was on a business trip in Australia after his wife passed away. My own career was on pause, or maybe it had slammed into a wall.

Miri was quiet.

The kind of quiet where the silence hums louder than traffic.

Where you can hear the thoughts *behind* your thoughts.

One evening, I sat in a dimly lit room, the balcony doors open to the night.

A movie played softly in the background.

Nothing unusual.

And then,

a voice in my head:

"Jump from the balcony."

I froze.

It didn't sound like me… and yet, it did.

No drama, no panic, just a *terrifying stillness* and a single, sharp command: *End it.*

I stood. Walked toward the balcony.

The concrete below looked peaceful. Almost… *inviting.*

Then, something inside split.

One part of me leaned toward the edge.

The other, the *silent witness*, simply watched.

That observer saved me.

The feeling lingered for 2–3 days, like a scent that wouldn't wash off.

Months later, back in Vietnam, jobless again, *hollow*,

the voice returned.

"Tie a rope. Jump from the balcony."

I even heard it, the imagined *thud.*

But again, the witness rose.

A softer voice this time:

"No. Just observe. Don't act."

Around then, a friend asked, "What do you want to do now in life?"

I said quietly, "I feel my mission is over on planet earth."

It wasn't despair.

It was a strange… completion.

Like a man with his bags packed, waiting at the station of existence.

My wife noticed it too.

“It feels like you’re preparing to go home,” she said,

“Not this home… the *real Home.”*

And then it hit me.

I was 45.

Exactly the age I had once joked about.

That throwaway line from my youth had been a seed.

And somewhere between all the years of living, losing, and longing, that seed had grown into a storm.

Sacred Pause and Reflections

- How much do the *things you say, even in jest, influence your path in life?*
- How conscious are you of the seeds you plant through your *beliefs, words, and desires?*

Psychological Lens

Psychologically, this story reflects how **fragmented parts of the psyche** can surface in unexpected ways. What appeared as a passing wish was actually the voice of a *split-off part* seeking recognition. In **Internal Family Systems (Richard Schwartz)**, these parts are not pathological but protective, holding unprocessed emotions, unmet needs, or frozen memories. Their surfacing is less about danger and more about an invitation to *integration*.

The central existential question, *"Who am I?"*, is also alive here. Stepping into the stance of an **observer** rather than identifying fully with the wish aligns with what **Viktor Frankl** called the "space between stimulus and response," where freedom and choice reside. From that space, I could connect the dots, see the underlying vacuum, and begin to understand this not as impulse but as a fragmented self—reaching for wholeness.

Another layer here is the power of **language and suggestion**. Cognitive psychologists like **Albert Ellis** and later, **Aaron Beck** emphasised how our words and thoughts shape beliefs and lived reality. A casual phrase may not manifest immediately, but when vulnerability is high, it can resurface with surprising force. In **Buddhist psychology**, this is mirrored in the story of **Mara**, the tempter who waits for the psyche's most fragile moments to strike.

Ultimately, this experience became a form of what Alexander and French described as a **corrective emotional experience**. The wish was no longer a dangerous impulse but a message: a part of me longing to be seen, understood, and reintegrated. Healing came not by suppressing it, but by holding it with *compassion and awareness*, filling the vacuum not with action, but with presence.

Symbolic Meaning

Symbolically, even a casual wish is rarely *casual.* The playful thought of "living only till forty-five" may sound like a joke, but it can also be a mask, a *defence mechanism* concealing an *old wound.* Humour here becomes a veil, protecting what feels too raw to name directly.

Such wishes often arise not to declare fate, but to fill the *vacuum* left by *unhealed pain.* They are like patchwork stitched over a tear, fragile, temporary, yet pointing us toward the deeper absence beneath. In this way, the wish is both *cover and clue*: it hides the wound, yet symbolically reveals where the healing is most needed.

The *balcony scenes* are powerful symbols. A balcony is a *liminal space*, neither fully inside nor outside, much like a state of mind: between living and leaving, between attachment and detachment. The *"observer self"* that intervenes represents the *Higher Witness*, the timeless aspect of consciousness that can interrupt conditioned impulses.

The wife's comment about "preparing to go home" ties into **transpersonal psychology**, where death is reframed not as an end, but as a return. In this lens, the "mission is over" feeling signals not physical death, but the death of an *old identity* or *soul contract*, making space for a new phase, if the person chooses to stay.

41. The Box of Kajal

When I was young, I watched a TV serial. I don't remember its name, but one episode stayed etched in my mind.

A young woman married into a wealthy, traditional family. She loved wearing *kajal (eyeliner),* but in her new home, this was forbidden by custom.

Months passed. She stopped wearing it. The light in her eyes *dimmed*.

One day, her husband noticed her unhappiness and decided to "fix" it.

He bought her a beautiful kajal box, presented it proudly, and walked away, satisfied that he had restored her joy.

She quietly set the box aside and went to sleep.

The episode name was *Astitva*, meaning "existence." I didn't understand the ending. My father explained:

"He first took away her existence by forbidding what she loved. Giving her a box later doesn't restore it, because her *freedom to choose* was already stolen."

That story stayed with me because it revealed how love, when bound by control, can lose its essence. I began noticing this same pattern in small, everyday moments around me.

A friend once brought me sweets his mother had cooked. I liked them and said so. From that day on, every time he visited home, he brought me sweets, because I had told him, *"I like them."*

I only liked them that day, not every day. But I never told him. I just kept eating them.

Sometimes, what people think is kindness is actually an imposition wearing a smile.

It isn't the gift that matters; it's whether you were *free to want it* in the first place.

And yet, another layer of truth glimmers: I can still be grateful that my friend always thought of me, even if the sweets became *a quiet burden.*

Gratitude transforms the weight, because gratitude is the fastest way to raise my own vibration.

Sacred Pause and Reflections

- What is your *"kajal", a small act of self-expression you stopped to fit in?* What *tiny step* would restore it today?
- When have you silently accepted the *"sweet"*, something given repeatedly, rather than *naming your real preference?* What words could you try *next time*?
- How might you hold both *truths* at once: *honest communication* about your needs and *gratitude* for the *intent* behind someone's care?

Psychological Lens

At first glance, this story looks like something small, even trivial, a tiny cosmetic box, a question of choice, a gesture of control. But what is being played out is one of the most subtle and common dynamics in intimate relationships: the tension between *autonomy and conformity.*

Moments like these invite us to reflect on the deeper truth hidden in ordinary gestures: the fine line between *love and control,* between giving freely and giving what we think the other wants. The question isn't about kajal itself, but about whose voice matters and whose choice defines the moment.

This story captures the subtle but powerful dynamics of autonomy, consent, and disguised control in relationships. From the lens of **Self-Determination Theory (Deci & Ryan)**, one of the core human needs is autonomy, the ability to make choices about our own lives. When someone first forbids and then later "gives" you that same choice, autonomy isn't restored. Instead, the act becomes symbolic of control, not care.

Psychologists sometimes call this **benevolent control**, when behaviours are framed as help or kindness but subtly undermine freedom. The husband buying kajal after forbidding It's a perfect example: the gift doesn't erase the earlier deprivation; it reinforces who holds the power to grant or withhold.

Over time, such patterns can create **conditioned obligation**, the silent compliance that comes from not wanting to reject someone's "thoughtfulness." Like the sweets I once ate without wanting to, the kajal becomes less about preference and more about harmony. This is how emotional resentment begins to build beneath the surface.

On a deeper level, repeated experiences of overridden autonomy can slip into **learned helplessness (Seligman)**. When personal choice is consistently dismissed, whether in small things like cosmetics or larger life decisions, a person may stop asserting their needs altogether. The unspoken belief forms: "Why speak up, if it won't matter?"

So, the box of kajal isn't really about make-up. It's about the lifelong negotiation between intimacy and individuality, between being loved and being free. The real wound isn't about beauty, but about *belonging*: whether my choices are seen as my own, or only valid when permitted by another.

Symbolic Meaning

The three key objects in this story are not random details; they are *archetypal symbols* carrying deeper meaning.

Kajal Box – It represents identity, self-expression, and the freedom to choose how one presents themselves to the world. To forbid it's to deny that freedom; to later return it without restoring true choice is like giving back an empty shell.

Sweets – They symbolise *recurring obligations* disguised as kindness. Something small and once-pleasant can quietly turn into a burden when imposed repeatedly. The sweets become less about nourishment and more about silent compliance.

Together – The kajal and the sweets mirror two sides of the same truth: imposed care is never true care. One reflects how *autonomy* can be taken away under the guise of *love*, the other how obligation can grow under the guise of kindness. Symbolically, they warn us about the illusion of restored freedom and the hidden cost of repetitive obligation.

And yet, with awareness, both can be alchemised: receiving care with gratitude, while reclaiming the freedom to choose, which is where true intimacy begins.

From death's silence, only one force rises strong enough to endure: love.

Chapter Seven

The Unfolding of Love

"Love isn't the reward for healing; it is the soil in which healing grows."

42. Under the Goddess's Watch

Saints, pujaris, tantriks, they were part of the air I grew up in. Our home always seemed to hum with *mantras*, carry the scent of *incense*, and hold the footsteps of holy men who claimed they could read destinies, unearth gold, or bend fate with a ritual.

One of them had a temple far away, tucked in the folds of hills. My mother asked me to visit.

I left at 4 p.m., thinking I'd be back the next day.

By 9 p.m., I had only reached the nearest junction, just in time to learn the last bus to the temple had gone. A lone van agreed to take me partway.

The road dissolved into darkness.

Lightning lit up trees bending under a storm.

Rain poured so hard the world blurred.

The van stopped in the middle of nowhere for twenty long minutes. My heart thudded; no mobile phones back then, no way to call for help. Finally, it rolled on, dropping me still 4–5 km from the temple.

The rain was relentless. Paddy fields lay between me and the hill path, impossible to cross at night. I found shelter in a small bus stop, barely a structure. Somewhere nearby, beyond the curtain of rain, I knew a river ran past a *cremation ground.*

I opened the food my mother had packed for the temple priest and ate a little. Hours passed. The rain softened, but the night was thick and blind. I decided to stay.

At some point, I noticed him, an old man lying on the bench beside me. He had not been there before. Almost naked, skin like paper, eyes half-closed.

I stayed awake all night, yet felt no fear. Only a strange, *calm knowing* that I wasn't alone.

At 4 a.m., I saw a small temple nearby. I walked over and poured water on the *Shiva linga*, the earliest prayer I had ever offered in my life. It felt like a gift only this strange night could give me.

By sunrise, I climbed up to the main temple. They were worried; my mother had been calling all night on the landline. They told me they had sent someone down to look for me, but he'd found nothing.

When I reached back home later, my mother told me of her dream:

The *goddess* of that temple came to her dream that night, holding a lantern and saying,

"Don't worry. I am taking care of your son."

Sacred Pause and Reflections

- Do you find it easier to trust in your *own strength,* or to *surrender to the care of something beyond you?*
- Have you ever sensed *a presence you couldn't see, yet felt safe with?*

Psychological Lens

That night at the bus stop, with thunder rolling, rain pouring, and cremation grounds just steps away, fear could have swallowed me whole. And yet, what surprised me was the calm that eventually settled, as if an *invisible hand* held me in place. Psychologically, this touches on **attachment to a protective figure**. **Attachment Theory (John Bowlby's, 1969)** explains how, in times of distress, the mind instinctively seeks a *"secure base."* For me, that base became the *imagined presence of the Goddess*, an internalised figure of protection that anchored my nervous system when everything around me suggested danger.

There's also the phenomenon of **transitional objects** (**Donald Winnicott, 1953**). Children often use a blanket or toy to soothe themselves, but adults, too, can carry symbolic anchors of safety. In my case, the temple, the dream my mother had, and the sense of divine presence became that transitional object, bridging the gap between fear and security.

Neuroscience frames this differently, through the concept of **neuroception** (**Stephen Porges, 2011**), the unconscious detection of safety or danger. Even though logic told me I was vulnerable, my body read subtle cues, the shelter, the old man nearby, the ritual of offering water to Shiva at dawn, as signals of safety. These cues shifted my nervous system out of *fight-or-flight* and into a fragile but real state of regulation.

What I realised later was that this was also an encounter with what **Carl Jung** called the **archetype of the Great Mother**, the timeless symbol of nurture and protection. She appears in dreams, myths, and rituals, often when the psyche feels exposed or abandoned. My mother's dream of the Goddess assuring her of my safety wasn't a mere coincidence; it was the psyche weaving myth and reality into a *holding environment* for both of us.

In the end, the night became less about surviving danger and more about discovering that safety isn't always the *absence of threat.* Sometimes it's the *presence of an unseen holding*, a reminder that even in isolation, one isn't fully alone. And this, at its deepest level, is the *essence of faith.* Faith binds us when logic breaks down. Faith keeps us moving when fear would rather paralyse us. Faith is that *invisible thread* that allowed me to sit through the storm, to wait out the darkness, and to believe that the dawn would come.

Symbolic Meaning

The goddess is the archetypal **Great Mother (Jung)**, nurturing, sheltering, but also capable of fierce discipline. Her *"watch"* represents the soul's awareness that nothing in life is truly hidden; it can be a source of *alignment* or an oppressive reminder of our perceived shortcomings.

The constant gaze can symbolise **moral vigilance**, an inner call to live in integrity even when no one else is present. But it also warns of the shadow side of devotion: when faith turns into *self-policing*, authenticity can shrink under the weight of imagined divine disapproval.

The deeper insight: the goddess's watch isn't just about being judged, it's about being *witnessed*. And sometimes, the transformation comes when we shift from fearing that gaze to feeling *held* by it.

43. The Healing Touch

When I was a child, I watched a television series on *Gautam Buddha.*

One episode introduced *Angulimaar,* a feared bandit who had just become Buddha's disciple.

In that episode, they were walking through a jungle when they came upon a pregnant woman, doubled over in *labour pain.* Her groans filled the air.

Buddha turned to Angulimaar and said,

"Place your hand on her head."

Angulimaar froze.

"But… I only became your disciple yesterday. How can I *heal* her?"

Buddha simply repeated,

"Place your hand on her head."

And when he did, she found relief instantly.

I remember sitting cross-legged before the TV, eyes wide, heart thudding. *I want to do this too,* I thought. Just the *power to take someone's pain away.*

Years later, I found *Reiki.* I trained. Practiced. Helped many. People felt better. Energy moved. I became a *Reiki Master.* But still, I kept asking:

Is there a power I can carry all the time? One that doesn't need symbols or rituals? Something constant?

The answer came quietly, like something I had always known: *Love.*

The seed of this understanding was sown by that Buddha story I had seen as a child.

But seeds don't bloom overnight.

This one was nurtured slowly, through years of searching, failing, healing, and unlearning.

Each experience softened me, stripped me, opened me a little more.

And when the heart finally opened, I could see the *vast potential of love*.

Not as an idea, not as a fleeting feeling, but as a *living force*, steady, supernatural, limitless.

Love is the only true supernatural power.

It doesn't need your hands, only your presence.

It doesn't require technique, only that you see someone *fully, without judgment, with kindness.*

And often, that alone can lift pain.

That is the power I carry with me now.

Sacred Pause and Reflections

- How do you usually respond when you *cannot fix someone's pain;* do you *withdraw, overdo*, or simply stay present?
- What does *"healing"* mean to you? Is it *curing, relieving, or simply walking alongside?*
- What is a story from your life where you felt the *power to take someone's pain away,* not by a physical act, but by a *simple* act of *presence*?
- What holds you back from *offering love freely, fear of not being enough, or fear of being too much?*

Psychological Lens

This moment of healing reflects **co-regulation** (**Stephen Porges, polyvagal theory**): our nervous systems influence one another. When one person offers grounded presence, the other's body shifts from distress toward safety.

The *healing touch* wasn't just physical; it was the nervous system's way of saying: *"You are safe. You are not alone."*

Trauma research reminds us (**Bessel van der Kolk**) that many wounds are *preverbal*, stored in the body. *Attuned touch and presence* can bypass the thinking mind and reach those hidden layers, helping to reintegrate what was once fragmented.

Neuroscience confirms this: when we feel loved, stress hormones drop, oxytocin rises, and the body opens pathways for healing. As **Gabor Maté** emphasises, trauma heals in *attunement*, the felt sense of being deeply seen and accepted.

For me, this is the shift from *sympathy* to *unconditional positive regard* (**Carl Rogers**). Sympathy reacts to pain; love is a constant presence. It asks nothing; it simply sees. The true miracle isn't *doing* but *being*.

Symbolic Meaning

Symbolically, the healing touch is a *bridge*, from isolation to connection, from suffering to belonging. Hands across cultures are archetypes of care and agency. In Jungian terms, a hand placed with love represents the *Self* reaching out to restore *wholeness*.

The story also echoes the *wounded healer archetype* (**Jung, Henri Nouwen**): those who have known pain often become vessels for healing others.

And across traditions, love is remembered as the highest force:

- Christianity calls it the greatest commandment.
- Sufism sings of love as union with the Divine.
- Buddhism teaches compassion (*karuṇā*) as the balm for suffering.

For me, the symbolic, psychological, and spiritual truths converge here: *love is ordinary and supernatural at once.*

So, is love enough to be a supernatural power? Yes, but not in the way my child-self imagined. Not as instant magic, though sometimes miracles occur. Rather, It's the miracle of presence: to sit so fully with another that their pain feels held, their humanity honoured, their existence safe.

That is the power I choose now:

Love as energy. Love as medicine. Love as the bridge between the visible and the invisible.

And in this sense, yes, love is more than enough.

44. Love is Real

Massage places in India have a reputation.

Ask anyone and you'll hear the same thing, whispers about *"happy endings"* that, in truth, are not really happy at all.

I'd always been curious.

Not for what the rumours promised, but for the experience itself. Could it be as seedy as people claimed? Or could there be something more human hidden in the folds of it?

One day, I decided to find out.

I chose an expensive place, partly to avoid the grimy, neon-lit picture in my mind, partly because of the name: *Moksha.*

It was tucked away in one of Delhi's upscale neighbourhoods, the kind where the air feels different. Inside, it was quiet, almost temple-like, with the low hum of a fountain in the corner.

After paying at the reception, an older Chinese or Japanese woman greeted me.

She led me to a pair of stools near the fountain. Without thinking, I sat on one, only to realise I'd chosen the masseuse's seat instead of the client's. We both laughed. Ice was broken.

She washed my feet, a gesture intimate in its simplicity, then guided me into the massage room.

Her hands were steady and skilled, unlocking knots I didn't know I carried. Halfway through, I asked for a head massage. She didn't understand, so she called in the manager, who walked in with cautious eyes, almost suspicious. I explained. The air softened, and I got my head massage. Bliss, not the hushed kind people gossip about, but the kind that leaves you *lighter, softer, more like yourself.*

Years later, I moved to Gurgaon.

By then, massage parlours had multiplied like weeds after the monsoon, some even lined up inside malls. I decided to try again, to return to that small island of stillness I'd once found.

But this time was different.

The place smelled faintly sour, the lights were too dim, and the walls were tired. I was in the middle of a messy divorce, endless court hearings, accusations, and the feeling of *running without arriving*. I just wanted an hour where the world couldn't find me.

That's when I met her.

She was from the Northeast. Quiet. Gentle. And *wary*. More than once, she asked if I was a police officer. I asked for her number so I could return to her next time, but she refused.

Later, I learned why.

The industry worked like a shadow economy, rotating staff to avoid suspicion, coded offers, and constant fear of raids.

By chance, I found her again months later, in another parlour. This time, she remembered me. We talked. She told me about her family, the constant moving, the pay cuts, and the unspoken rules. And eventually, she gave me her number. From then on, I'd text her before visiting.

On some visits, we didn't even do a massage.

We just sat in that dim room and talked. She listened without trying to *fix me*, without *judgment*. I learned more about her than most clients ever would: her hometown, her dreams, her quiet resilience.

One day, hollowed out by loneliness, I asked her something I'd never asked anyone in such a place.

Not sex.

Not desire.

"Can you just... love me?" I said softly. I was so empty inside and alone that I wanted someone to love me.

She didn't flinch.

She sat beside me, placed her hand on my head, and kissed my forehead.

At that moment, she didn't see me as a client. She *saw my pain, my emptiness, my longing,* and she held it without expectation, without fear.

That day, in the most unlikely of rooms, I found something real.

Something human.

Something that wasn't *for sale.*

Sacred Pause and Reflections

- When was the last time you truly *felt love in a hug, a cuddle, or simply sitting beside someone?*
- Have you ever experienced a season in *life* where you felt *deprived of love,* and *longed deeply* for someone to be by your side?
- What *small gestures, a touch, a word, a presence, have reminded you that love is real?*
- If *love were standing next to you* right now, how would you recognize it?

Psychological Lens

Looking back, I can see more clearly now what I felt then.

This story reflects the shift from **conditional regard** to **unconditional positive regard (Carl Rogers)**. Most of us grow up learning that love must be earned, through good behaviour, achievement, or meeting expectations. What I received that day was *non-contingent love*: the sense of being worthy simply because I exist.

From an **attachment theory** perspective, this was a **corrective emotional experience**. In that dim room, I touched the feeling of **secure attachment**, a bond where my value wasn't dependent on performance. For someone carrying the weight of rejection and divorce, this moment was deeply *reparative.*

Her quiet presence wasn't clinical, but it was healing. Neuroscience shows that **authentic connection** activates the **ventral vagal system (polyvagal theory**), lowering stress hormones, raising oxytocin, the chemistry of trust and safety. My body learned at that moment: "It's safe to relax. I am held."

The heartbreaking question, "Can you just… love me?" is a raw, vulnerable plea that is met not with a transaction, but with a pure act of kindness. This genuine connection triggers a physiological response. Neuroscience tells us that this kind of **authentic love** and **presence** activates the **ventral vagal system** (as described in **polyvagal theory**), reducing stress hormones and increasing **oxytocin**, the neurochemical of bonding and trust. In that physiological state, the body learns, "It's safe to relax. I am held." The story, therefore, isn't just about a search for human connection, but a profound discovery that *love is a real,* *measurable*, and deeply *healing power* that can be found even in the most unlikely of places.

Symbolic Meaning

Symbolically, that forehead kiss was a *sacrament*.

It wasn't romantic, not erotic; it was *recognition*.

In Jungian terms, it felt like an encounter with the **Anima archetype,** the inner figure of compassion and wholeness that restores balance when the psyche feels broken. In that moment, she mirrored not just who I was, but who I longed to remember: someone lovable even in emptiness.

The story is also a living echo of the **wounded healer archetype;** her own life of hardship allowed her to meet my vulnerability with tenderness, not judgment.

For me, it became proof that *love is real*, not in fantasy, not in rumour, but in a lived, embodied act. Not in grand gestures, but in a hand on the head, a forehead kiss, a presence that whispers:

"*You are enough,* even when you bring nothing but yourself."

45. The Bag of Infinite Nuts

I was travelling alone from Vietnam to India.

No wife beside me, no heavy tiffin boxes filled with apple slices, crackers, or oranges. Normally, she packs so much food that I complain about the extra bags, and then, ironically, we eat almost none of it.

This time, it was just me. Light baggage. Empty stomach.

Sitting at the airport, I rummaged through my laptop bag and found a small, familiar packet of nuts. My wife had bought them for me once, and I'd slipped a few in "just in case." I smiled at my foresight, opened it, and ate slowly, savouring each bite.

But when I finished, I was still hungry.

And I knew there were no more. I'd checked the bag before. Empty.

Still… something in me stirred.

I remembered a story my wife once told me about a woman who manifested exactly the money she needed from an empty purse.

She told me about *Cynthia Sue Larson* and the concept of *"high-energy money"*, how the universe responds to faith, alignment, and attention rather than frantic effort or fear. She explained that abundance often appears not through force, but through *playful trust*: when you relax into *possibility* instead of *scarcity*, the resources you need often reveal themselves in unexpected ways.

The idea made me laugh.

“Alright,” I told myself, “Let’s try.”

I closed my eyes for a moment, not in deep meditation, not with effort, but with a *quiet, playful faith.* Then I reached into the bag.

My fingers brushed against something.

Another packet.

Another packet.

I froze. Goosebumps.

I pulled it out slowly, almost afraid it would vanish. But it didn’t. I opened it, still smiling in disbelief, and ate again, this time tasting not just the nuts, but the mystery.

When I finished, I wanted to test my faith again.

Surely, I thought, this is where it ends.

I reached in…

One more packet.

I sat there at the airport, staring at my bag like it was a magician’s hat.

It wasn't about the nuts.

It was about *trust.*

About the possibility that what you truly need might already be there, just waiting for the moment when you reach with *faith instead of fear,* as Bell (my wife) had taught me.

Sometimes, life hides little miracles in our bags, not to feed our hunger, but to *feed our belief.*

Sacred Pause and Reflections

- When have you discovered that something you once carried as *"baggage"* actually became *nourishment* or *wisdom* later on?
- Have you ever carried food or something "just in case" and later noticed how it felt like both *baggage* and a *resource* at the same time?
- If this packet of nuts were a symbol, what *hidden abundance or resource* might you already be carrying *without realising it*?
- When in your life did you feel *you didn't have enough,* yet later discovered you *actually had more than you thought*?

Psychological Lens

As I held that little packet of nuts, I realised it was more than food. It was an enactment of something deeper, *a parallel world where resources are never scarce, where one bag could open the door to unlimited bags, if only I reached with faith instead of fear.*

From a psychological perspective, the bag of nuts wasn't about hunger or scarcity at all; it was *about abundance*. It showed me how the mind itself shapes experience: when fear is present, the bag feels finite; when faith is present, it becomes infinite. **Stephen Covey** describes this as the **abundance mindset**, the belief that there is always enough, and that life expands when we trust it.

Rather than a symptom of grasping, I began to see my reaching as an *exercise in belief.* The bag became a mirror of the power of mind: *scarcity thinking* contracts reality, while *faith* opens it. This is more than positive thinking; It's a psychological shift from *fear-driven control* to *trust-driven openness.* In that sense, the nuts were never just food; they were a *manifestation practice*, a reminder that provision comes not from *clinging*, but from the *willingness to receive.*

At the same time, **Kahneman & Tversky's** idea of **loss aversion** helps explain why the pull toward clinging feels so strong. Our minds are wired to fear losing more than they celebrate gaining, which makes trust difficult. Here, abundance isn't denial of that wiring; It's the *conscious choice* to soften it, to let faith override the bias of fear.

Melanie Klein's object relations also illuminate this moment. The "bag of infinite nuts" symbolised not just food, but the *fantasy of an inexhaustible caregiver*, the wish that comfort and provision will never run out. As an adult, that fantasy can still linger. Yet instead of binding me to dependency, the bag invited me into trust: to internalise abundance not as endless external supply, but as an inner stance of *sufficiency*.

Bell's (my wife) sharing about manifestation added another layer of clarity. She reminded me that manifestation isn't magical thinking, but a psychological shift, from *compulsion to curiosity*, from *anxious grasping to playful reaching*. In this way, the nuts became more than food; they became a practice in faith, an enactment of the power of the mind to transform scarcity into abundance

Symbolic Meaning

Symbolically, the bag isn't about lack at all; It's about the *source* we believe in. If we see the source as *scarce*, we receive little; if we see it as *infinite*, we allow ourselves to receive more. The bag becomes a mirror of our *faith*: the limit is never in the supply, but in our willingness to trust.

In Indian mythology, the *Rishis* could manifest anything instantly in their hands. They understood that what we need already exists in the fabric of reality. From a *quantum perspective,* time isn't *linear but layered;* everything already is. What feels like "waiting" is only our mind's attachment to sequence. When that dissolves, provision can appear instantly.

The deeper invitation of the bag is to shift from clinging to trusting, from waiting to receiving. Its message is simple: *"The source is infinite. You are already provided for. You are already enough."*

46. A Thousand Flowers

I was living with my cousin in Delhi, during a season of uncertainty. She guided me through the process of applying for the Company Secretary course, a professional program that trains individuals in corporate law, governance, compliance, and financial management, while I found solace in my daily prayers at a nearby temple to Lord Shiva, asking for guidance and clarity amid the unknown.

One day, my parents stumbled upon a crumpled piece of paper near a cow dung heap. It listed an MCA college in Chandigarh. They followed the lead, reached out to a family acquaintance, an editor at a reputed magazine, and within days, I had admission.

Grateful beyond words, I made a quiet *vow* to Shiva: I would offer him a *thousand flowers* from his sacred plant.

During my post-graduation, I often cleaned the temple as *seva*. Those small acts of service brought peace, structure, and a sense of purpose. Yet I knew that my promise to Shiva was waiting, an intentional gesture of gratitude that required both patience and devotion.

In the middle of the course, I boarded an almost-empty bus from Chandigarh to Delhi, with a mix of anticipation and nervous excitement. At the next stop, a young man got on. With so many seats free, he chose the one beside me.

We spoke easily, and to my surprise, the conversation turned toward Shiva, his stories rich, personal, as if he knew exactly why I was travelling; everything he was sharing about Shiva.

A strange certainty rose within me: *This is no ordinary man.* A quiet voice inside whispered, *Shiva himself has come to meet you.* Then, as suddenly as he had appeared, the man rose when the bus paused on the way to Delhi.

He turned to me, offered a gentle blessing, and stepped off, leaving me with the sense that *something divine* had just passed through my life.

When I reached Delhi the next morning, I gathered the flowers early in the morning, bathed, and went to the temple where I had made my vow. As I began to chant Shiva's 108 names, I noticed a woman smiling at me from across the courtyard.

Wherever I moved, she seemed to appear again, by the shrine, near the steps, under the shade of a tree.

She came to me and asked what I was reciting. Then, with childlike sincerity, she requested that I say the name again so she, too, might receive the blessing of Lord Shiva. I sat down and began to chant the sacred names aloud for her. But to my shock, after only a line or two, the words slipped away. I forgot them completely, the very words I had been reciting faithfully for more than ten years.

I tried again and again, but after ten or twelve names the chant would vanish from my mind. At last, I gave up. She looked at me with a gentle smile and said softly,

"Perhaps Shiva doesn't want me to hear them today. Maybe it isn't *yet my time to receive his blessing."*

Her calmness, her serene smile, it felt *strangely mystic*, just like the man on the bus. As if she were teasing me, yet carrying the presence of something divine. She rose, walked a few steps, while I sat there still caught in confusion. And then, suddenly, the names returned to me.

Excited, I turned to call her back so she could hear, but she was gone. *Vanished.* I searched for her everywhere, but she was nowhere to be found.

Sacred Pause and Reflections

- Have you ever found yourself at a *crossroads* where your *future felt uncertain?* How did you seek *guidance or grounding*?
- What is the *"temple"* in your life today, the *place, practice, or person* that helps you *return to yourself when uncertainty feels heavy*?
- How might your *daily routines* carry hidden meaning, if you looked at them *symbolically rather than practically?*
- What *"symbols"* or *"love languages of life"* show up in your *spiritual path*?
- When you pause and look back, can you recognise how *invisible forces, divine, ancestral, or relational,* have shaped your *direction*?

Psychological Lens

Psychologically, this story reflects what **Alexander and French** described as a **corrective emotional experience**. Forgetting Shiva's names wasn't a lapse of devotion but a *divine interruption,* a playful reminder that blessing isn't tied to *flawless performance.* What once looked like failure became *grace*, strengthening my faith and showing that I was already on the right path, held by *divine timing*.

It also revealed the shift from **transactional love to transformational love**. Transactional love says, *"If I do this perfectly, then I am worthy of blessing."* Transformational love whispers: *"You are already blessed, already enough, even in imperfection."* In psychological terms, this was a dismantling of **perfectionism** and the move toward **surrender**, letting go of control to rest in presence.

The encounter also pointed to **Sacred Immanence**, a principle in **transpersonal psychology:** the divine isn't confined to rituals or conditions but present in every being, every moment. The woman's smile, her gentle words, carried that essence. To see the divine in another is to let compassion itself become a spiritual practice.

Even the language of love appeared here. **Gary Chapman's love languages** teach us that love is expressed in different ways: words, service, gifts, and presence. Forgetting the chant showed me that divine love doesn't depend on one "language" alone. It can reach us through silence, interruption, or even forgetting. What matters isn't *perfection in expression,* but *openness to receiving.*

Symbolic Meaning

Symbolically, this story is about the journey from *effort to grace.* The *thousand flowers* represent *devotion*, the human need to give, to prove, to fulfil a vow. Yet the *divine interruption of forgetting* showed that what mattered wasn't the offering itself, but the *heart behind it.*

The stranger on the bus and the woman in the temple appear as **archetypal messengers**, embodiments of *Shiva*, reminding me that the divine often arrives in ordinary forms. Their sudden disappearance mirrors the truth of spiritual encounters: they come briefly, shift us deeply, then vanish, leaving only the *imprint of presence.*

Forgetting the sacred names symbolises *surrender*. It was as if Shiva himself was saying: *"Stop clinging to words, stop striving for perfection. See me in the moment, see me in her smile."* The vow of flowers, then, was never about numbers or ritual, but about opening the eyes of the heart.

In the end, the story reveals a movement from **transactional love**, "If I give enough, I will be blessed", to **transformational love**, "Blessing is already here." The flowers dissolve into *presence*, the names dissolve into *silence*, and the divine shows itself in the simple act of seeing God in another.

47. The Cave of Surrender

Today, I had the rare chance to sit in deep *hypnosis* with Greg, a French hypnotherapist.

I entered with a question that had quietly followed me for years, like a shadow I could never turn fast enough to see:

Why, despite all my clarity, insights, and spiritual work, do I still find myself surviving... instead of building?

Something invisible, yet ancient, felt as though it was holding me back.

Greg's voice guided me inward until my mind became still.

Suddenly, I was standing in a dense, ancient forest. In front of me, a cave, quiet, humble, timeless. I walked toward it and stepped inside.

There, seated in perfect stillness, was a man in orange robes, his long beard resting on his chest. His eyes were closed, yet I felt seen, utterly and completely.

It was *Yogi Ram Paramhans.*

This was no symbol, no invention of my imagination. His presence was as real as the ground beneath my feet, rooted and radiant, ancient and familiar. I didn't need to speak. My soul was already in conversation.

Greg's voice broke the silence:

"What do you see in your *left hand*, your *survival side*?"

I looked down.

A *Yoga Danda* rested there, the wooden staff used by monks.

It was *discipline. Endurance.* The years of holding myself together, balancing, and persevering.

"And in your right hand, your future side?"

A *Shankh* appeared, a sacred conch shell, luminous and alive. It was the call of new beginnings, the invitation to create from truth, to step forward with sacred intention.

"Now," Greg said gently, "allow both hands to come together… and merge into your heart."

As they met, a surge of energy pulsed through my chest. It was as if lifetimes folded into a single moment, survival and creation becoming one.

Then Greg's next words landed like a prayer:

"Place your hand on your heart and repeat:

'I allow myself to stop *surviving*.

I allow myself to *build*.'"

The words didn't just echo in the room; they sank into my bones. *The survival mode, once necessary,* now loosened its grip. In its place, the builder within rose quietly, but with a calm authority I had not felt in years.

Greg asked:

"What does your future-self want to tell you?"

I turned to the Yogi. He didn't move, but his *silence thundered.*

And then, the message came, without sound, yet undeniable:

"Rise in love."

Not fall. Not flee. Rise.

Rise in vibration, in responsibility, in creation, in alignment.

And finally, Greg asked:

"If this integration were complete, if you truly began, what would your next step be?"

Without hesitation, I answered:

"I will start again."

And Yogi Ram Paramhans, still in stillness, sent his final blessing through the silence:

"Tathastu. Tathastu. Tathastu."

(So be it. So be it. So be it.)

Sacred Pause and Reflections

- If you stepped into your own *"cave"* today, what burden would you be willing to *finally lay down?*
- What do you resist *surrendering* most, *control, certainty, or the image of who you think you should be?*

Psychological Lens

For me, this journey revealed something I've long known in theory but rarely felt so viscerally: the need for **inner integration.**

Psychologists like **Carl Jung** would call it the **union of opposites**. In my hypnotic vision, the "left hand" (survival mode) and the "right hand" (building mode) embodied two distinct **ego-states**, two life strategies that often pulled me in different directions.

Survival mode aligns with **Maslow's** lower tiers: safety, security, and endurance. It was symbolised by the **Yoga Danda**: discipline, structure, perseverance.

Building mode aligns with the higher tiers: self-actualisation, creativity, purpose. It was symbolised by the **Shankh**: the sacred call to begin anew.

By merging these two, I experienced what psychology would describe as **ego-syntonic integration**, the reconciliation of parts that once seemed opposed, now learning to coexist and empower one another. In other words, what once felt like a **split self**, punctuality as integrity versus lateness as disregard, was now being re-stitched into a coherent whole.

I also recognised traces of **learned helplessness (Seligman, 1975)**. Years of setbacks may have conditioned me to expect survival as my ceiling. In hypnosis, though, the imagery worked as a *corrective experience:* survival was reframed not as a prison, but as the foundation upon which creation could finally rise.

When I placed my hand on my heart and repeated, *"I allow myself to stop surviving. I allow myself to build,"* it functioned both as a **cognitive reframe** and a **permission statement**. In therapeutic terms, this is akin to **narrative re-authoring**, rewriting one's internal story from endurance to authorship, from limitation to agency.

The insight was clear: the conflict was never just about survival versus building. It was an **identity–value conflict**. I had long valued resilience, but I also longed to create. Until both were allowed to exist in me, I could never feel whole.

Symbolic Meaning

Symbolically, the forest and cave are classic **threshold spaces**, portals between the *conscious* and *unconscious*, often appearing when a hero is ready to meet their deeper truth. The bearded yogi embodies the **Wise Old Man** archetype, a Jungian symbol for inner guidance and timeless knowledge.

The Yoga Danda symbolises **support and discipline**, a staff that helps maintain balance, much like survival patterns that keep us alive in difficult times.

The Shankh (conch) is rich in Hindu symbolism, often associated with the voice of creation, the call to dharma, and the start of auspicious ventures. Merging these two items mirrors the **alchemical marriage**, the blending of the practical and the spiritual, the earthly and the transcendent.

The yogi's message, "**Rise in love**," inverts the common phrase "fall in love", shifting love from a state of surrender into a state of ascension and conscious empowerment.

This reframing echoes **transpersonal psychology**, where love isn't just emotional attachment but an elevated state of being that aligns with purpose and contribution.

Finally, the repeated *"Tathastu" ("So be it")* acts as a ritual seal, similar to the final chord in music, that signals completion of an initiation. It affirms that the transformation isn't just imagined but *accepted* by the deeper self.

48. The Staircase and the Book

There are moments in life when we don't want advice.

We don't need another conversation, distraction, or list of possibilities.
We need *clarity*, from somewhere beyond the usual noise.

That night, I wasn't looking for a friend or a partner to talk things through.

I was seeking something else entirely,

a guide, a whisper, a sign.

So, I closed my eyes and began to meditate.

A *golden spiral staircase*, ancient, glowing, endless.

I began to climb.

The air grew lighter with each step, and yet something in me felt heavier, like I was carrying questions too large for words.

Halfway up, I saw my friend Florence sitting quietly on a step.

"Come with me?" I asked.

She smiled, her eyes warm but resolute:

"It isn't *my time yet*."

I kept climbing.

A few steps ahead, my friend Aanchal sat, hands resting in her lap.

"Walk with me?" I asked again.

She shook her head gently.

"I've been there before. This part is *yours*."

I climbed alone now, the steps curling upward into a light I couldn't see the source of.

Finally, I reached a room.

It was filled with relics, wooden chests, silver bowls, scrolls whose edges looked older than memory itself.

And in the centre stood a man.

Long white beard. Eyes like deep water.

The kind of presence that makes you feel both completely seen and slightly unworthy.

I asked him my questions.

He answered in riddles.

Then, as suddenly as he appeared, he began to leave.

"Wait," I called after him. "I have more to ask."

He paused, tilted his head, and raised one hand.

In it, a book.

Love Is a Choice.

A single red-and-white leaf on the cover.

I reached for it. And in that instant, my eyes opened.

I was back in my room, breath quickened.

I grabbed my laptop and searched,

And there it was.

An actual book. By Robert Hemfelt. On relationships, patterns, and healing.

I sat still, the quiet electric around me.

I hadn't climbed a staircase into the clouds.

I had climbed into myself.

And the bearded man wasn't a stranger.

He was my *own wisdom*, dressed in the image of someone I'd trust enough to listen to.

The answer had been simple all along:

Love isn't something that just finds you.

It's something you *choose*,

in silence,

in doubt,

even when no one else is ready to walk beside you.

Sacred Pause and Reflections

- When you think about your own journey, who are the *"friends on the staircase",* the ones who can walk with you for a while, but *cannot take the next step for you*?
- If a book were waiting for you on the *next step* today, what do you *secretly hope it would reveal?*
- Have you ever looked *outside for guidance,* only to realise the *wisdom was already inside you*?

Psychological Lens

This story is a vivid example of the **active imagination** process described by **Carl Jung**, the conscious use of imagery and inner dialogue to connect with parts of the psyche that hold insight.

The spiral staircase is a classic psychological symbol for **inner growth and individuation**; it doesn't go straight up like a ladder but circles, reflecting how real transformation is rarely linear.

The figures met along the way, friends who choose not to continue, may represent **internalised voices of others** or aspects of the self that are not ready for the next level of change. The "bearded guardian" is an archetypal figure, similar to what **Joseph Campbell** called the **Wise Old Man** in the Hero's Journey, a personification of inner wisdom that appears when the seeker is ready to hear a deeper truth.

Receiving the book *Love Is a Choice* connects the imagery to **agency in relationships**. From a psychological standpoint, this moment may mark a shift from **attachment-driven expectations** ("love will find me") toward **self-determined intimacy** ("I choose love consciously").

The unconscious mind used the image of a tangible book to anchor the insight, bridging symbolic meaning with actionable reality.

Symbolic Meaning

The spiral staircase is a timeless symbol of the **ascent toward higher consciousness**, but its curve also means that at every turn, you momentarily lose sight of the top. This mirrors the nature of psychological work, periods of clarity followed by uncertainty, all part of the same climb.

The friends who don't come along reflect the **inevitable shedding of companions** when moving into new phases of self-discovery; some people's journeys align only for certain stretches.

The book itself is a **sacred object archetype**, much like the "Book of Life" in various mythologies. In dreams and visions, books often symbolise *knowledge you already hold within yourself*, waiting to be opened. That it had a real-world counterpart reinforces the Jungian idea of **synchronicity**, meaningful coincidences that signal alignment between inner and outer worlds.

Ultimately, the staircase and the book together tell a simple but profound truth: *wisdom is climbed toward, not handed over; and love is chosen, not stumbled into.*

49. The Angels in the Traffic

I was moving homes, from Gurgaon to Noida.

A *new job*. A *new apartment*. A *new chapter* waiting to be lit.

But in my family, entering a new home isn't just about shifting boxes.
It's about timing. Energy.

Lighting that first *diya* at the *exact* right hour so blessings arrive before the furniture does.

That morning, I was already behind schedule.

Between Gurgaon's gridlock and Noida's unpredictable roads,

my chances of reaching "on time" were shrinking with every red light.

And then I remembered something from years ago,

a practice I'd once trusted with my whole heart:

working with angels.

No incense. No elaborate ritual.

Just a simple conversation with the *unseen*.

So, I whispered:

"Angels, Angels, Angels help me. Clear the way."

Then I smiled, got bolder:

"No red lights. No traffic. Partway like I am your only task today."

I wasn't pleading.

I was speaking like a child who knows their parents will always show up.

And then… the magic began.

Green after green after green.

Roads are unusually clear.

No honks. No chaos. Just flow.

I wasn't driving anymore.

I was being *carried.*

I reached the new place *exactly* on time.

The diya lit with a single match, flickered once,

then stood still.

Like it knew it was home.

Was it a coincidence?

Or a *superpower that only wakes when you believe without flinching?*

You don't always have to move the universe.

You just have to trust that it's already moving with you.

It works best when *doubt takes the back seat*,

and *trust holds the steering wheel.*

Sacred Pause and Reflections

- Who are the *"angels"* in your life right now, the *unexpected people* or *moments* that remind you that *you're not alone*?
- If there were *an angel* in your *traffic* today, what message do you imagine the angel might be whispering to you?

Psychological Lens

This story illustrates the concept of **cognitive reframing**, deliberately shifting the mental lens through which we perceive an event. Instead of focusing on the inevitability of traffic delays, the narrator engages in a **faith-based intervention**, invoking "angels" to clear the way. Psychologically, this taps into the **locus of control** and **self-efficacy**, the belief that one's actions (or prayers) can influence outcomes.

From a **positive psychology** perspective, the act of calling on unseen support isn't just superstition; it can *reduce anxiety*, *increase optimism*, and create a mental state that's more open to noticing opportunities (in this case, green lights and clear roads). Neuropsychology also suggests that when belief is paired with vivid imagery, the brain responds as though the outcome is already in motion, *aligning perception and action* toward that result.

The narrator's tone, "I wasn't pleading. I was speaking like a child who knows their parents will always show up", reflects **secure attachment dynamics**. People with a history of dependable caregivers often find it easier to trust unseen or abstract sources of support later in life.

Symbolic Meaning

Traffic here operates as a *metaphor* for *life's blockages,* delays, red lights, and congestion, symbolizing *external constraints.* Calling upon "angels" invokes the archetype of the **divine helper**, a figure found in nearly every mythic tradition, from guardian spirits to animal guides, who clear obstacles so the hero can proceed on their path.

The absence of honks and chaos mirrors the *inner stillness* that can emerge when one surrenders control to a higher order, be it divine, universal, or simply a deep trust in timing. Lighting the diya at the exact moment becomes a symbolic act of *alignment with cosmic timing,* the idea that certain actions hold more potency when done "in the right moment," much like planting seeds in the right season.

The closing insight, "It only works when *doubt takes the backseat* and *trust holds the wheel*", is both literal and archetypal. The vehicle becomes a *chariot of trust,* moving through the unpredictable currents of life without resistance.

50. The Urge to Watch

Today, I caught myself noticing my son hiding again.

In the back seat of the car, he angled his phone away from me.

Later, while sketching, he quickly closed his notebook as I walked past.

A part of me wanted to rush into his room, check his school bag, scroll through his phone, to see what he's watching, who he's texting, what he's carrying out with him.

Where does this urge come from?

A memory surfaced, an old friend.

Bold. Lively. Fearless.

She once fell in love with a man from a very different world.

He was a car driver; she came from a wealthy family.

She spun lies, twisted stories, and found a hundred ways to hide her meetings from her parents.

Eventually, she married someone else.

Last time I saw her, she seemed happy.

But I've always wondered:

Will she one day watch her own daughter with suspicion, not because of her daughter's actions, but because of her own memories?

That question turned back toward me.

What about my own past?

What did I hide?

What am I still hiding from myself?

Is my unease about my son's secrecy really about him?

Or is it the *echo of my own shadow*?

The version of me who once kept things tucked away, away from the eyes of those who cared?

Maybe I am not really scanning *him* at all.

Maybe I am scanning my own history.

Maybe the urge to watch isn't *control*, but a *mirror*, reflecting the parts of me I still don't trust.

Sacred Pause and Reflections

- If the *urge to watch* is also an *urge to learn,* what truth *about yourself* might be hiding in the things you *cannot look away from*?
- What is one thing you've done in your life that *no one else knows,* and do you notice an *urge to sneak its trace* into your children, friends, or the spaces you keep hidden, like a diary or phone?

Psychological Lens

The urge to watch, in my case, wasn't about idle curiosity; it was about *control*. If I kept my eyes on what was happening, then I couldn't be blindsided. Watching meant staying one step ahead, reducing the *chaos that comes from uncertainty*. It was as if my gaze itself could act as a *shield*: "If I see it, it cannot surprise me."

There was also pride in this position, a quiet *defiance*, a sense of power in saying: *"You are not making a fool of me. I know what you are doing."* This knowing gave me dignity. Even when I couldn't stop something, the act of naming it, of being aware, restored a piece of my *agency*. In psychological terms, this borders on **displacement**: instead of wrestling with my own vulnerability or powerlessness, I displaced that energy into the act of surveillance. Watching became both *armour and weapon*.

But beneath the surface lies another layer: the *fear of repetition*. Having done things in the past that I regret, a part of me unconsciously projects that history forward: *"What if my children are walking the same path? What if they repeat my mistakes?"* So, the watching takes on a moral weight: it isn't just about control, but about *prevention*, an anxious attempt to *interrupt the cycle* before it repeats.

From a family systems lens, this can be seen as **intergenerational vigilance**: the unresolved guilt of one generation manifesting as hyper-attentiveness in the next. Watching, then, becomes not simply about others; It's about keeping my *own shadow* in check, mirrored through those I fear may repeat it.

Symbolic Meaning

The act of watching from the shadows evokes the archetype of **the sentinel**, the guard at the gate. In mythology, the sentinel protects, but also limits freedom by deciding what passes and what stays hidden. Here, the "gate" is the son's privacy, and the father stands in the ambiguous space between *protector* and *intruder*.

The "hidden phone" and "sketchbook" function as **symbols of the inner world**, places where identity, desire, and self-expression are forming. When these are shielded, it can signify not only rebellion but also the sacred process of **individuation** (**Jung**). To interfere too soon risks disrupting the natural unfolding of the child's psyche.

The story's final reflection, that "maybe it isn't about my son at all", is the *pivotal insight.* It acknowledges the **shadow self** (**Jungian concept**): the parts of us we've disowned but continue to project outward. Until the narrator faces his own unresolved secrecy, the urge to watch will remain, not as a response to his son's behaviour, but as an echo of his own unexamined past.

51. The Trembling Chariot

After completing my post-graduation, I stayed with my cousin's sister for a while. My life felt like a long, echoing *waiting room,* no job offers, no exams to study for, no clear direction.

When the outer world gives me no answers, I've always turned inward. To the divine.

Every morning and evening, I'd sit cross-legged before the small wooden temple in their home, lighting incense, chanting *mantras*, whispering gratitude into the still air. If I couldn't move forward, I could at least move closer... to *something greater than myself.*

One evening, as I sat in prayer, something unusual happened.

The temple began to tremble.

At first, it was a faint *vibration*, like the hum of a distant train. Then it grew stronger.

Inside, a small silver *chariot* began to shake. The statues of the deities quivered in unison, as if they too had been caught in some invisible current.

My first thought was an *earthquake.*

But the ground under my feet was perfectly still.

The air was thick, but silent.

Fear found me.

I called out to my cousin's son, a tall man who could cross a flight of stairs in seconds.

He appeared in the doorway, and in that very instant, everything stopped.

No tremor.

No vibration.

Just a stillness so complete, it made me question whether I had imagined the whole thing.

I told the family. They were startled, but no one could explain it.

Three days later, my cousin's sister left the house. She and her husband separated.

Over the next few years, their family *unravelled*, ties loosened, bonds dissolved, and the home I had known as warm and whole slowly became a place of *absence*.

It was only much later that I came across an old belief: when the goddess's chariot trembles on its own, it's a sign of *approaching upheaval*, a *bad omen* whispered through divine hands.

And even now, I wonder why I was chosen to witness it.

Perhaps it was a warning.

Or perhaps it was just the universe's way of reminding me: sometimes, knowing the storm is coming doesn't help you stop it.

It only makes you watch the first dark cloud roll in, and stay awake until the last drop of rain falls.

Sacred Pause and Reflections

- When life gave you a sign, did you treat it as *fate*, or as an *invitation to awareness*?
- When life *chooses you* for something that not everyone sees, how do you *feel*?
- How do you hold *moments of mystery*? *Do you explain them away,* or *allow them to change the way you see*?

Psychological Lens

From a psychological perspective, this story sits at the intersection of **premonition, meaning-making, and cognitive pattern recognition**. Human beings are wired to seek patterns, especially in ambiguous events. When something uncanny happens, like the temple trembling without explanation, the mind instinctively links it to later events, a process called **retrospective meaning-making** (**Michael Shermer** refers to this as "**patternicity**").

At a deeper emotional level, witnessing such a moment can create what's known in trauma psychology as a **vicarious shock**, an experience that, while not physically harmful, imprints itself because it challenges our sense of normalcy. You didn't just hear about the bad omen; you *saw* it. That direct witnessing creates a more persistent memory trace, often accompanied by **anticipatory anxiety** in the months or years after.

The follow-up family breakdown then fits into a psychological loop called **confirmation bias**: once an event is labelled as a "sign," the mind interprets subsequent, even unrelated, ev*ents as proof of its truth.* This reinforces belief and can subtly alter behaviour, sometimes making us more guarded, more passive, or even resigned to what we think is "fate."

Symbolic Meaning

In symbolic terms, the *trembling chariot* in Hindu tradition carries profound weight. The chariot is often linked to **divine movement**, as in the chariot of the goddess or the chariot in the

Bhagavad Gita. When it trembles, especially without human touch, it can be read as a *disruption in divine order*. Symbolically, this becomes the "*earthquake in the heavens*" that foreshadows instability in the human realm.

The fact that the shaking stops when another person enters introduces the motif of **the chosen witness**, a common archetype in myths and mystic experiences. In such stories, the divine or supernatural event is shown to one person (often the sensitive or spiritually tuned) and *concealed from others.* This creates both a gift and the psychological weight of a *silent burden,* knowing something that others cannot or will not fully understand. burden: to hold knowledge that others cannot fully understand.

The subsequent family *unravelling* parallels the chariot's trembling: what was once stable (relationships, unity) begins to shake until it cannot hold together. The event becomes both a literal memory and a **symbolic prophecy**.

And perhaps the deeper symbolism is this: sometimes the divine trembles not to warn us of the storm ahead, but to remind us that even stability is temporary. The chariot doesn't shake forever; it quivers, and then it stops. So too with life: upheaval comes, passes, and leaves us to find *meaning* in what remains.

52. Twenty-Five KG Baggage

After my first marriage ended, I waited ten years before I found someone, I truly wanted to build a life with. Then came the move to Vietnam.

My home in Gurgaon was a humble two-room apartment, but inside it… years of accumulation. Things which I had moved from house to house without ever opening. Books I always unpacked first and packed last, as if they were my *anchor* in every storm. Objects untouched for years, yet somehow still claimed as part of me.

The airline rules were clear: *25 kg check-in baggage + 7 kg* hand luggage. Every extra kilo would cost fifteen dollars.

That night, March 31st, 2021, I stayed awake, surrounded by piles of possessions. The irony struck me in a cold wave: in life, too, we pay a price for carrying *extra baggage*.

I began to weigh each item, and my back began to ache from the repetitive strain. I'd put a pile on the scale, see the weight, and then, filled with a *frantic indecision*, start taking things out, only to second-guess myself and put them back. It was a *physical manifestation* of a decade of indecision.

Sitting before my bookshelf, my heart sank. Beside it, a large white Buddha statue stared at me with an unblinking calm. On a small table, my Buddhist *altar*, where I had chanted for years, waited. The walls were covered in sticky notes from my restless mind, ideas for books, stray thoughts, and collections of coins. I looked at all of it and felt the *weight of every memory* attached to every object.

It had taken me years to understand that the heaviest load wasn't in these boxes or suitcases. It was in the *attachments*, the *memories*, the *unresolved emotions* I'd been hauling for decades. A quiet truth rose in me: *You need to be lighter if you want to fly.*

So, I began to release. Item by item. Memory by memory. I picked up the Buddha statue, ran my hand over the cool, smooth stone, and set it aside to be given away. I dismantled the altar and carefully packed the sticky notes into a folder, deciding to leave the tangible collection of my old ideas behind. *Letting go of things that no longer served the life I was walking into.*

When I finally boarded that flight, my bags were within the airline's limit. But more importantly, my soul was lighter. After a night of struggle, I finally closed the last bag. I was teary, slowly closing my eyes and breathing deeply. On one side, I was leaving so many things and memories behind; on the other, there was the pure joy of meeting someone I loved, the beautiful, new life waiting for me.

I carried only three things that didn't need weighing: *Love. Peace. Contentment. Detached from the past. Engaged in the present.* Ready for what was waiting ahead.

And in that moment, I realised: the decisions we take, however uncertain, are always right, because they carry us forward into the unknown.

Sacred Pause and Reflections

- What *"extra baggage"* are you carrying that *no longer serves your next chapter?*
- Which *possessions, memories, or identities* have become *too heavy* to keep moving with?
- If you had only *25 kilos of your life* to carry forward, what would you choose?

Psychological Lens

On the surface, this story is about airline baggage limits. But beneath it, it becomes a striking *metaphor* for the *psychological weight we carry* in life. The 25kg check-in baggage and the 7kg hand baggage are not just travel rules; they mirror how we divide our *burdens*: what we openly place on the conveyor belt for others to see, and what we keep closest to us, carried in silence.

Psychologists describe something similar in the concept of **emotional baggage**, the unresolved past experiences, beliefs, and wounds we carry into present situations. Unlike luggage, there's no counter to weigh it, yet it shapes every step of the journey.

There's also a dynamic here of **cognitive load** (**Sweller, 1988**): the more mental and emotional weight we carry, the less capacity remains for presence, joy, and spontaneity. Even when the airline says "you are within the limit," the body knows when it's not.

From a relational perspective, this story resonates with **family systems theory** (**Bowen**). Often, the heavier suitcase is filled not just with our own stuff but with inherited roles and expectations, what families, cultures, or societies hand to us as "must carry." The smaller hand baggage, ironically, often contains the most precious or fragile parts of us: the *private fears, the secret grief, the hidden longings* that never leave our side.

And here's the irony: we often obsess about the outer baggage, the big visible load, while it's the "7kg hand baggage", the intimate, unspoken truths, that weigh most on our hearts.

Symbolic Meaning

This story reads almost like a *dreamscape*, where every object carries *archetypal weight*. The *25kg + 7kg limit* isn't just an airline rule but a *cosmic reminder:* you cannot carry everything forward. In Jungian terms, It's the *Law of Exchange:* to step into a new phase of life, something must always be left behind.

The **bookshelf** becomes more than storage; it represents *memory, knowledge, and identity*. Each book left behind feels like abandoning a fragment of self, a past voice that once shaped you. The **two-room set** mirrors the *psyche itself:* one room filled with stories and attachments still useful, the other cluttered with obsolete identities waiting to be released.

Even the **baggage fee** has a symbolic echo; It's the *emotional or spiritual cost* of carrying unresolved attachments forward. Every extra kilo demands a price. The question becomes: What are you still paying for that you no longer need?

The **flight to Vietnam** is no mere relocation. It's a *rite of passage,* a *border-crossing* both external and internal. Vietnam itself carries an archetype: *resilience* and *rebirth*. A land that endured colonisation, wars, and unimaginable suffering, yet rises again and again to flourish. For someone arriving, Vietnam whispers: "You too can be *reborn*. You too can grow new roots in the ashes of what you leave behind."

The movement from **India to Vietnam** is also a shift in consciousness. India, with its ancestral weight, represents depth, tradition, and the karmic inheritance of millennia. Vietnam, by contrast, radiates youthful dynamism, rapid change, and the invitation to experiment with becoming. Symbolically, this migration isn't just geographical but metaphysical: a *shedding of* *heavy ancestral* patterns in exchange for lightness, possibility, and renewal.

In the Jungian language, this moment at the airport is a **threshold ritual**. Boarding the plane wasn't just about travel; it was an initiation. A letting go of skins too heavy to carry, and the first step into a rebirth waiting on the other side.

The mask falls, the silence breaks, the rage cools, the body softens, death whispers, and love remains, not as an answer, but as the presence we carry forward.

Epilogue: The Healer's Mirror

Healing never really ends.

It simply changes its *language*.

What once arrived as *pain becomes a teacher; what once felt unbearable becomes a doorway.*

There was a time when I believed healing meant reaching a place where nothing hurts anymore. Now I know—it means learning to *walk with what still does*, *tenderly and wisely*. It means holding our wounds not as proof of our *suffering* but as evidence of our *capacity to feel, to grow, to love.*

Every story in this book began as a whisper in the dark. They were moments of *being lost*, moments of *remembering*, moments of seeing myself in the mirror of another's pain. Somewhere along the way, I realised that being a *"therapist"* was never about fixing others. It was about learning how to *sit beside pain*—mine and theirs—without *turning away.*

Healing isn't the absence of pain; It's the *presence of meaning.* It's the return of breath after the storm, the quiet recognition that what *broke you* also *built you*.

And perhaps, in the end, being a *wounded therapist* simply means learning how to *love what once felt unlovable*—within and around us.

May these stories remind you that your wounds are not the end of the story.

They are the soil in which your wisdom grows.

May you meet yourself again and again—with *gentleness*, with *curiosity*, with *awe*.

To Be Continued…

These pages may have an ending, but the story doesn't. Healing isn't a destination; It's a *path we keep walking,* sometimes in circles, in leaps, always discovering new layers of ourselves.

Every story you read here was a moment in time, a *snapshot* of who I was and what I understood then. Tomorrow, my *truths may deepen*. Yours may *shift*. That is the beauty of being human: we are never finished.

There are deeper parts of me still *hidden, untouched, unspoken,* waiting in the quiet corners of my being. I am *mustering my courage* to bring them into the light. I know those stories will demand more *honesty*, more *vulnerability*, and more *surrender* than I have yet dared to offer.

I don't know what the next chapter will hold.

Perhaps more stories.

Perhaps more silences.

Perhaps the same lessons, learned in new ways.

What I do know is this:

I will keep *listening to life,* to the subtle whispers beneath the noise, and to the *wounds that keep shaping the therapist* in me.

And maybe, somewhere in the pages yet to be written, our paths will meet again.

Until then…

Let's keep *walking*. Let's keep *watching*. Let's keep *becoming*.

The Practice of Healing

If you wish to take this journey beyond these pages, begin simply.

Healing isn't a method; It's a *practice of presence.*

Here are three doorways:

1. **Awareness:** *Seeing Without Judgment*

   Notice what is alive in you right now. Not what should be there, but what *is.* Awareness begins the moment you stop trying to be better and start being honest.

2. **Allowing:** *Letting It Move Through*

   Every emotion has a rhythm. Grief wants to be held. Anger wants to be heard. Joy wants to be shared. Let them pass through without *resistance*—they are all visitors from your own soul.

3. **Alignment:** *Acting From Truth*

   Healing stabilises when your actions begin to match your inner knowing. Speak kindly, rest deeply, love bravely. Let your choices be *prayers in motion.*

   And remember—progress in healing isn't measured by how calm you look, but by how *tenderly you can meet your storms.*

Gratitude Beyond These Pages

Thank you for walking this journey with me.

If these words have touched something within you, may they remind you of your own *strength and softness*—the *quiet wisdom* already living in you.

May your path be kind.

May your wounds become mirrors.

May your heart remain curious.

With Gratitude and Angelic Blessing,

Ankur

References & Inspirations

This book draws its wisdom from the intersection of psychology, spirituality, and lived human experience. Deep gratitude to the teachers, thinkers, and seekers whose work continues to illuminate the path of healing, love, and awakening.

Psychology, Healing & Human Behaviour

- Bowlby, John. Attachment Theory. Basic Books, 1969.
- Frankl, Viktor E. Man's Search for Meaning. Beacon Press, 1959.
- Hemfelt, Robert; Minirth, Frank; & Meier, Paul. Love Is a Choice. Thomas Nelson, 1989.
- Schwartz, Richard C. Introduction to Internal Family Systems. PESI Publishing, 2020.
- Svagito R. Liebermeister. The Roots of Love: A Guide to Family Constellation. Osho Media International, 2010.
- Svagito R. Liebermeister. When Life Stops. Osho Media International, 2016.

Spirituality, Consciousness & Love

- De Angelis, Barbara. The Choice for Love: Entering into a New, Enlightened Relationship with Yourself, Others, and the World. Hay House, 2015.
- Ikeda, Daisaku. Unlocking the Mysteries of Birth and Death. Middleway Press, 2004.
- Osho. Being in Love: How to Love with Awareness and Relate Without Fear. St. Martin's Griffin, 2008.
- Wolynn, Mark. It Didn't Start with You: How Inherited Family Trauma Shapes Who We Are and How to End the Cycle. Penguin Books, 2016.

Buddhist & Philosophical Wisdom

- Nichiren Daishonin. The Writings of Nichiren Daishonin, Vol. 1 & 2. Soka Gakkai International, Tokyo.
- Jung, Carl Gustav. The Archetypes and the Collective Unconscious. Princeton University Press, 1968.

About the Author

Ankur Nag is a therapist, coach, and facilitator dedicated to guiding individuals toward healing, awareness, and authentic living. With a Master's degree in *Counselling Psychology* and over two decades of professional experience, Ankur brings a rare balance of corporate insight and deep therapeutic wisdom to his work.

While spending 21 years in the IT industry—serving in leadership roles including Vice President of Operations and Agile Coach—Ankur was simultaneously practising as a therapist and facilitator. Over the years, his passion for human transformation deepened, leading him to integrate his corporate experience with his therapeutic and spiritual path. This unique blend allows him to approach healing with structure and clarity, and leadership with empathy and consciousness.

As a Certified Hypnotherapist, Family Constellation Facilitator, Reiki Master, Past Life Regression Therapist, Mindfulness Coach, Transactional Analysis Practitioner, and trained in various other transformative modalities, Ankur has worked with individuals and groups across Asia, helping people heal emotional patterns, rediscover purpose, and reconnect with their inner truth.

During his journey, Ankur met his wife and soulmate, Bell Tran—an Executive Coach, Trainer, and Inner Child Therapist. Together, they founded *ankurbell.com*, where they share their mission of spreading awareness about mental health and emotional well-being. As partners in both life and work, they design and deliver corporate wellness programs, leadership trainings, and mental health workshops, helping individuals and organisations move toward greater consciousness, connection, and balance.

Blending the precision of a strategist with the compassion of a humanist, Ankur believes that every life challenge is an invitation to awaken. His work continues to inspire many to lead with presence, authenticity, and love—in their personal lives, relationships, and leadership journeys.

If you wish to contact the author, you can reach him through the details below:

✉ **Email: ankur.naag@gmail.com**

🌐 **Website: ankurbell.com**

"The outer world transforms when the inner world begins to heal."